CHOICE
IN DYING

CHOICE IN DYING

The Facts about Voluntary Euthanasia

Jean Davies

WARD LOCK

Ls9, 8241 179. 7

For Jack and Edith

A WARD LOCK BOOK

First published in the UK 1997
by Ward Lock
Wellington House
125 Strand
LONDON
WC2R 0BB

A Cassell Imprint

Copyright © Jean Davies 1997

All rights reserved. No part of this publication may be
reproduced in any material form (including photocopying or
storing it in any medium by electronic means and whether or
not transiently or incidentally to some other use of this
publication) without the written permission of the copyright
owner, except in accordance with the provisions of the
Copyright, Designs and Patents Act 1988 or under the terms of
a licence issued by the Copyright Licensing Agency,
90 Tottenham Court Road, London W1P 9HE. Applications for
the copyright owner's written permission to reproduce any
part of this publication should be addressed to the publisher.

A British Library Cataloguing in Publication Data block for
this book may be obtained from the British Library

ISBN 0 7063 7510 6
Typeset by Falcon Oast Graphic Art
Printed and bound in Great Britain by Biddles Ltd

Contents

Jean Davies's interest in the subject of voluntary euthanasia goes back many years. In 1980, as a committee member of the British Voluntary Euthanasia Society, she attended the international conference at which the World Federation of Right-to-die Societies was inaugurated. In 1984 she became editor of the World Federation Newsletter, and in 1988 she was elected vice-president, becoming president in the following year. In Britain she was chairman and chief spokesperson of the VES from 1985 to 1990, and she has lectured widely, both in the United Kingdom and abroad. She currently holds the post of president of the European Division of the WFRD.

Foreword

One of the bleakest things to happen to me is the unexpected telephone call that shatters my peace of mind and causes me untold distress. Such phone calls, which are quite frequent now, did not happen at all until I became a shadowy part of the VES, the Voluntary Euthanasia Society. Once it became known that I was associated with the society, even though only remotely, I seemed to become an 'instant authority' on assisted death. These phone calls are from people who beg me to help them end the life of someone to whom they are very close – a wife, husband, lover, parent, child. Pain has reached such a point in their loved one's lives that they desire only its ending, even though this means the ending of that life itself. And there is absolutely nothing that I can do.

As you will realize as you read this excellently researched book, I can do nothing to help these desperate people. I cannot even suggest how the suffering might be ended, because that would be 'aiding and abetting' suicide, which is illegal in England and Wales. Usually these telephone calls are made to me when the caller has reached the end of his or her tether or, more often, when the patient has reached that point. The despair is intense, the pleas are heartbeaking, and yet still one is unable to help.

More often than not, I pass the caller on to the staff in the VES office. Like me, they will be able to offer only the same vague comfort, but they have a calmer, more professional manner, and speaking to one of the members of the VES staff will have a far more reassuring effect than pleading with a friend for help.

This book is, tragically, full of case histories of people in circumstances similar to those confronting the people who contact me. Some of these stories are almost unbearably painful to read. But the book is helpful even if, in the end, the outlook is so bleak, if only because, through reading it, readers will feel less alone and, perhaps, a little less helpless.

You will find in this book a specimen form for an 'advance directive', which will be of great value to family and friends, quite apart from the help it offers to any doctors involved. The directive *must* be drawn up when the person to whom it applies is in good health, and it must be witnessed by at least two independent witnesses. Even the completion of an advance directive, however, by no means guarantees that a doctor will assist, for no one can force doctors to break their oaths, and the phrase 'voluntary euthanasia' can make many people, including doctors and nurses, react in the opposite way to what is intended and mutter: 'It all smells of Nazi Germany, to me.' It is so easily and so often overlooked that the word 'voluntary' means that it is an individual's personal wish to be eased, with dignity, towards their end.

It must not be forgotten that there are wonderful hospices, to which one may, if one is fortunate (for there are too few of them), be taken and cared for with easeful dignity and peace. However, it is important to remember that five per cent of hospice patients remain in great pain; not everyone's agony can be eased, and this is always admitted, as I have personally discovered, with the greatest possible distress by those who are involved with the hospice movement.

A book such as this, therefore, can be of only the greatest interest and help. It is timely in the extreme.

Dirk Bogarde

Introduction

Death will come to every one of us sooner or later – none of us has any choice about that. By the end of our own lives, however, most of us will have been involved, more or less closely, in the slow dying of a loved relative or friend, and many of these people will have wanted the sad process brought to a gentle end. Some deaths are much more unpleasant and lingering than others, and this is where the possibility of choice comes in.

If the incurably ill and suffering person reaches the stage of wanting to forgo the last stage of a dwindling life, it is hard for carers to find a good reason to refuse that wish. A reluctance to face saying 'goodbye' for the last time, although natural, is obviously putting one's own feelings first. Compassion and respect for the other person's right to self-determination should convince carers to respond to the dying person's last request. However, the law at present totally prevents them from doing so.

Choosing to die when confronted by a painful, long-drawn-out or undignified end – which is what voluntary euthanasia means – is often described as an 'emotive' subject. If by that we mean that it arouses our feelings, then, of course, it is. It would be a stony-hearted reader who did not feel overwhelming sympathy for the plight of some of the people whose circumstances are described in this book. The fact that a subject is emotive, however, does not mean that it cannot be discussed rationally. Nor does it mean that it is impossible to improve the law dealing with it.

The number of people who would actually ask for, and receive, help to die might be quite small, but what a comfort knowing that the possibility of choice existed would be to all those who think ahead and who like to be in charge of their own affairs. Those who prefer to take life, and death, as they come would be unaffected, and deaths brought about other than at the patient's wish would remain criminal acts.

No imaginary people or events have been described in this book, although most people have been given different names to protect their confidentiality. It has been a privilege for me over the years to listen to many of their stories, and to talk to them, their relatives and friends. Their stories are told to illustrate the many kinds of suffering that the present law imposes on those who are approaching the end of life. Some of the cases described show how a start has been made on finding a better way of coping.

Proper care of the dying is rightly regarded as one of the hallmarks of a civilized society, and that care needs to include the possibility of a chosen, dignified death.

Jean Davies

1

Does anyone really ask for help to die?

◇

'Tonight is a special occasion, Doctor.' The words were quietly spoken. Beatrice had congestive heart failure, and the disease had progressed to the point where she was dependent on oxygen to help her breathing.

'Why is that?' replied her doctor, preoccupied with preparing the injection she needed every evening to help her sleep and thinking of a birthday perhaps, even though she was 67 – not an age to be getting excited about a birthday, particularly in her state of health.

'This is the hundredth time you've come, and I think that is enough.'

'Whatever do you mean? Are you going to find another doctor?'

She would have laughed at that idea if she had had the strength. He had been her family doctor for many years, and they were on very good terms. 'No, I mean I would like a different injection, so that I wouldn't wake up tomorrow morning.'

He was obviously startled. 'But you know I am not allowed to do that.'

'Yes, I do know, but it is my dearest wish. Are you sure

you can't find a way?'

He promised to think about it and to talk to some of his colleagues, which he did. A few nights later he said, 'I will give you the injection you asked me about. Let me know when you are ready.'

'Oh, thank you, doctor,' she whispered. 'I have prayed for that.'

Let us think about some of the issues involved here before we find out what happened next. One is whether it was reasonable for Beatrice to ask for help to die. Did she have a right to contemplate an action that would bring about her own death? Even if she did have that right, was it wrong to involve someone else in helping her? And did her request not place the doctor in a dilemma, for he might have felt that it was his duty to continue treating her, despite her wish to die?

Many people learning of Beatrice's illness imagine that they, too, would feel as she did – that they had had enough of such quality of life. Being unable to move, struggling for every breath and entirely dependent on others for every physical need is not an enviable state to be in. Beatrice was being nursed at home by a loving family and with the help of visiting nurses, but even so, she had nothing to look forward to except the weeks or months it would take for her heart finally to stop beating.

But she was, of course, long past the point where she could end her own life, except by refusing food and drink, and she would need the cooperation of her medical carers for that to be a comfortable way to die. It would also take many weary days to take effect. Asking her doctor to help seemed to her the natural thing to do. After all, a doctor had helped her into the world and through every medical crisis since. The doctor replied that he was not allowed to do it, and according to law he was quite right. Nevertheless, if, after considerable thought, he decided that he would, he would then have to fill in a death certificate, including 'cause of death'. If he put 'congestive heart failure' that would not be true; it was going to be several more weeks of suffering before she died of that. But if he put 'so many mgs' of whatever drug he used, he could, and probably would, be charged with murder. This seems a cruel dilemma for society to impose on a doctor who is trying to do his best for his patient.

In Britain in 1935 a group of doctors decided that the position was intolerable. They set up an organization aimed at getting the law changed, giving it the imposing name, the Voluntary Euthanasia Legalisation Society. Beatrice certainly knew that her request to her doctor was voluntary. Her family had not suggested such a thing – in fact they took some persuading that it really was what she wanted. She might not have known the word 'euthanasia', even though it was what she was asking her doctor to arrange for her. Strictly speaking, it means a good death, from the Greek words *eu* (good) and *thanatos* (death). Since death itself is regarded as a bad thing by most people, it is sometimes translated as a 'painless' or 'peaceful' or 'merciful' or 'dignified' death, but the word also implies that this 'good death' has been deliberately brought about. It would not be used, for example, of someone who is found by his wife to be dead in the morning, having gone to bed apparently in full health.

During their years of power in Germany the Nazis misused the word 'euthanasia'. They introduced a system by which those people whom they thought unworthy to live were put to death, starting with the mentally handicapped. The mentally ill were soon included. These people were put to death quickly and almost painlessly, and so the Nazis called it 'euthanasia'. At no point, obviously, was the process voluntary. In 1941 the practice was stopped in the case of the mentally ill because of public objections, but by that time 70,273 people had been killed. This appalling figure had been overshadowed by the end of the war. The killing continued of homosexuals, political opponents, such as trade unionists and communists, and those persecuted for their 'race', the gypsies and, above all, the Jews. By the time the

3

full horror of the Holocaust was under way, the Nazis were calling it the 'Final Solution'.

This experience has meant that some people cannot use the word 'euthanasia' in its original sense. They become unable to discuss the subject of *voluntary* euthanasia rationally. For example, Bernard Levin, a prolific and highly regarded British journalist, has written quite frequently on the subject, and he always omits the word 'voluntary'. In 1989 he wrote an article in *The Times* called 'Under patient's orders – to kill'. A 92-year-old Dutch man, incurably ill and finding his life no longer endurable, had gone through all the necessary steps to receive help to die from his family doctor. The doctor had agreed to do it, but when the time came, he actually gave an injection of a tranquillizing drug. The patient woke, in dreadful distress, some hours later, and his son complained of the doctor's betrayal of trust. The Dutch Medical Disciplinary Board upheld the complaint, and the doctor was reprimanded for failing to keep his promise.

On this occasion Levin did not dispute the voluntary nature of the euthanasia, but his description of the case – 'a doctor being reprimanded (presumably a punishment only short of being struck off) for *not* killing his patient, with no better excuse than that the patient had indicated a wish to be killed' – pays no regard to the patient's suffering and his long-discussed decision to ask for help to die.

Spokesmen for the Roman Catholic Church also speak of 'euthanasia' as a system to be imposed on the dying without considering their wishes. They often link abortion and euthanasia, apparently unable to distinguish between the ending of the life of a foetus and the ending of the life of a suffering and competent adult at his or her own considered request.

The only ways of getting around the damage done by the Nazis to this Greek-derived word are by insisting on attaching the word 'voluntary' to it or by substituting a phrase such as 'help to die'.

Beatrice, of course, was not worried by terminology. She was now more relaxed, insofar as one can be relaxed while hooked up to a steady supply of oxygen, and felt comparatively cheerful because she now had something to think about. Talking was difficult because it used more effort than she could easily summon up, but thinking was something she could do.

'You know I've talked for a long time about how much I wish this was over.' She was speaking to her sister, Maria, also widowed, with whom she had been living for the last five years or so.

'Yes, and I wish you wouldn't. We're managing to look after you, aren't we?' The 'we' was mainly their sister-in-law, Helen, who lived not far away, and the team of visiting nurses.

'Of course you are. I'm very lucky. But it still isn't really living, and I'm tired of it.'

Maria began to cry because Beatrice was obviously serious, and although the nursing took up so much of her time and she hated to see her sister in such a poor state, they had always been on good terms. Now she was having to face saying goodbye and then going on, living alone. Beatrice cried a little, too. No one wants to die, even when they have decided they prefer to die rather than go on suffering indefinitely.

'I've spoken to the doctor and he says he will do it for me.'

'Oh, Beatrice! How could you do such a thing? You know he'll get into trouble, or he'll have to tell lies about it.'

'Being in my state makes you a bit selfish, Maria. I hadn't thought of it from his point of view. We'll have to talk to him again this evening.'

That evening the doctor explained that he intended to tell the truth, which would mean that the family could also speak openly about Beatrice's choice. She would be able to say goodbye to her chosen friends without having to guard her tongue about the future. Her decision would be far better for the family, but it might not be so good for him, so he would like to bring another doctor to confirm that, in the present state of medical knowledge, there really was nothing else to be done for Beatrice. The other doctor could also check that Beatrice was the one whose idea it was and that no one was trying to persuade her against her will.

Beatrice agreed. 'But I hope it will be soon, doctor,' she added wistfully.

'Tomorrow,' he promised. 'And I'll bring the drugs with me as soon after that as you decide. There is one more thing. I shall tell the police as soon as I have done it because I'll be breaking the law. They may want to come here. I'll ask them not to come in uniform with their sirens sounding, but I can't guarantee they will agree. How do you feel about that? I'm really asking you, Maria?'

'Will they be coming to arrest me?'

'No, no. I'm the one who will be the law-breaker. I hope they won't arrest me.'

'Well, I hope so too. Beatrice and I will need to talk about this some more, but tomorrow. She's too tired now.'

Maria brought Helen into the next day's discussion, and together they decided that a police interview following Beatrice's death was something they could face. Dr B, who was from another practice, agreed that medicine could do no more to improve Beatrice's quality of life, and, after talking to Maria, he was sure that the choice to die was being made by Beatrice herself.

By invitation, two close friends and neighbours called, one by one, the next day to say goodbye. That evening Beatrice said her final farewells to Maria and Helen, and she died in the presence of her priest. Her last words were of gratitude, to her doctor.

Because this happened in the Netherlands, and because the doctor had carefully followed that country's guidelines, he was not charged with any crime. At the time it could not have happened in that way in any other country in the world.

When deaths like this are described in magazine articles or discussed in television programmes, few people think it right that such a doctor should be regarded as a murderer in the eyes of the law. Most people in the audience or, if it is a phone-in programme, most of those who ring in, think that the law should be changed in this respect. On a wider scale, opinion polls also show that an overwhelming majority of people think the same. These polls have been conducted by nationally known, independent market research firms, including the Roger Poll in the United States, the National Opinion Poll in the United Kingdom and SOFRES in France. The same question has been asked in the United Kingdom as part of a National Opinion Poll survey, starting in 1969 and then at three- or four-year intervals thereafter. The question is: 'Some people say that the law should be changed so that a doctor can end the life of an incurably ill patient if that patient is suffering and has asked for that help in writing. Do you agree or disagree?'

The proportion agreeing with the proposition started at 50 per cent in 1969 and has risen steadily to 79 per cent in the most recent survey – four people out of five. That is in Britain. Polls asking basically the same question but worded slightly differently have been conducted in the United States and Canada, most countries of western Europe and most of the states of Australia. The results vary a little, but are never below 60 per cent and rarely above 90 per cent. In France in 1989, for example, it was 85 per cent in favour, and in Canada in 1991 it was 75 per cent.

Those who argue against such a change in the law have

difficulty disputing the evidence of these polls. One of the most often offered reasons for disregarding the opinions supported in the polls is: 'The question as stated is too complex for the man in the street to understand. The replies are therefore meaningless.' This is the same arrogant argument that was used against giving everyone the vote – the view that ordinary people are too stupid to be allowed to take part in choosing a government. In any case, if those replying really did not understand the question, the results of the polls would be muddled, sometimes for and sometimes against. In fact, it is remarkable how consistently they are in favour – and by a wide margin.

Another often-voiced objection is: 'How can you rely on opinion polls? Look what happens in the run-up to elections.' It is quite true that the replies given to a question such as 'How will you vote in the coming election?' bear little relation to the ways in which people do vote, but elections are often influenced by the most recent news headlines. Asking if a doctor should cease to be regarded as a criminal by helping an incurably ill patient to die with dignity, if that is what the patient wants, is a different type of question altogether, and is more likely to evoke a response such as 'My goodness, that's a choice I'd like to have when my time comes' or 'If only my poor mother had been able to get that help from her doctor. What a blessing that would have been!' or both.

A third attempt to deny the authority that the polls give to the movement that wants to decriminalize voluntary euthanasia is: 'Well, we can't have law-making by referenda, you know. If we did, capital punishment would be restored, and you wouldn't like that, would you?' Leaving aside the red herring about capital punishment, the first statement implies that those who want to legalize voluntary euthanasia want to do so by holding a referendum, which is not the case. Public opinion polls are quoted only to show that the statement 'most people support decriminalizing voluntary euthanasia' is based on substantial evidence.

Death is a familiar subject on our television screens. Books, films and television programmes about crime, usually involving murder, are among the most popular types of entertainment. Few things capture media headlines as surely as a sensational, real-life murder. But in all these cases, one element in our fascinated interest is the cosy knowledge that we are not personally involved. When it comes to deciding whether or not we want to legalize voluntary euthanasia, we may still think of someone else who is dying and what their wishes might be, but the memory of the death of a family member or friend, or even someone seen on television, seems to be what springs to mind, and that brings the subject much closer.

> Julia's husband was dying of a cancer that chiefly affected his digestive system. He had hospice-care nursing at home and would have liked to have died there. Unlike Beatrice, he had no doctor willing to break the law on his behalf, and he became so ill that he had to move into the hospice itself. 'Three weeks later,' Julia said, 'he died in my arms, and as he did so the contents of his stomach poured out of his nose. Was that a dignified death? Why did he have to endure those last three weeks of misery?'
>
> That was in England. Fiona from New Zealand described her husband's death. He was only in his forties but had an incurable heart condition and was very ill. He gave clear instructions that when his heart stopped he was not to be resuscitated. 'They resuscitated him five times,' she said, and the bleakness of her voice stunned those listening. He had died five times – let us hope with not much awareness – but she had to live with the memory of it.

People like Julia and Fiona would have liked their husbands to have been able to get help to a better death than they had, but they recognize that this was impossible as the law now stands. If they were asked by a market researcher conducting a poll on the subject, they would, of course, be among the four out of five people in favour.

It is worth noting that only about 15 per cent of patients who receive resuscitation, as Fiona's husband did, leave hospital alive, a figure that has emerged from recent large studies of the success of resuscitation in the United States and the Netherlands.

Few people, mercifully, have immediate experience of deaths in their family as unpleasant as Julia or Fiona had. The person dying may not, for example, have been in great physical pain.

Edith was 83 and living in an excellent nursing home. She had always been a most skilful needlewoman, and alarm bells had rung about five years earlier when she had knitted a sweater that was obviously and grotesquely wrong around the neck.

'That was what the pattern said,' was her defiant comment, challenging her daughter, also a good knitter, to think about why she had not corrected it, if the pattern was actually at fault. Edith had knitted countless garments from measurements alone and would, up to that point, have automatically corrected any misprint she found in a pattern.

It was the beginning of a brain deterioration that was never diagnosed as Alzheimer's disease, but the results were as devastating. She gradually lost her ability to exert muscular force. At first, this stopped her from using public transport because she couldn't climb on to the step of a bus or train. She had never driven a car, and although she could have afforded to take taxis, she had rarely done so and the thought did not occur to her. Soon her cooking was restricted. It is surprising how much effort you have to use to slice a carrot, and arms as weak as hers were now no longer able to open and close windows. Much worse was the loss of bladder control, eventually followed by loss of bowel control as well. After a long and horrible struggle to cope with all this in her own flat, she was moved, with her reluctant acquiescence, to the nursing home.

'If only I didn't wake up tomorrow morning,' she said as she settled down for the last time in her own home. A neighbour had been found dead in bed, not long before.

'But it doesn't often happen, love, does it?'

Mother and daughter were both widows, and the daughter was an only child, so there were only the two of them in this. 'No it doesn't. But you can't kill yourself, can you?'

'It isn't easy.'

The daughter was thinking: 'She's going to ask me to help her. What on earth am I going to do? How could I do it? How could I refuse to help her?' But she needn't have worried.

Edith's reply was: 'No, it isn't. And I'm not going to try.'

'Phew,' thought the daughter with relief. 'That lets me off the hook.'

But it didn't let Edith off the hook.

As soon as she got to the nursing home a catheter was inserted into her bladder, and she spent her remaining year with a urine bag fastened to her leg. She had always been a fiercely independent woman, and she found needing help to dress and keep herself clean humiliating beyond words. In fact, she spoke very little during that year. Her politeness never deserted her, and her complaints were confined to a comment, made only once: 'To think it's come to this!' It was quietly but bitterly spoken.

Both women had always been tremendously talkative, but the daughter found it increasingly difficult to think of anything to say. This was because her mother had always been full of her plans for the future, eagerly looking forward to and discussing the next event in her life, however trivial – planning the next piece of knitting or what to do next year in the garden. Although she had always read and watched television, she was much less interested in the present than in launching her next enterprise. Now there was no future to look forward to, and her interest in the present evaporated altogether. For the last six months she was unable to swallow solid food, so by the time the loss of muscular control reached her lungs, she was dreadfully emaciated, though still rational. During this time, one of the conversations with her daughter in the beautiful, non-smelly communal sitting-room had been as follows.

'What do you think about, sitting here all day?'

'I think about going to bed.'

'And what do you think about when you get to bed?'

'I think about going to sleep.'

'Not about getting up next day?'

'Oh no!'

If she had been allowed to stay in bed, Edith might have developed bed-sores, and so she was got up and dressed until the day before she died. At no point did she suffer physical pain, beyond the discomforts associated with a catheter, but her psychological pain did not bear thinking about. Her daughter's only defence was to try not to think about it. The fact that she could not cry or grieve when her mother died seemed to her an awful thing, but in truth, the person who was her mother had gradually died months before.

If the option of dying peacefully at home had been available, Edith would have accepted it gladly, and most people find little difficulty in sympathizing with the wish of people in circumstances such as Beatrice or Edith that they be allowed to have medical help to die.

But what about cases when the suffering person cannot ask? This makes the euthanasia involuntary, and as such it is not campaigned for by any of the worldwide societies that are working so hard to give us choice in dying. Deciding to end the life of someone who cannot give his or her consent seems a much harder problem yet, strangely enough, the courts in both Britain and the United States have tackled these cases first.

In April 1989 crowd control measures failed at a football match in Sheffield, and 95 people died in the crush. Almost four years later the last victim died, having spent the intervening time in coma. His name was Tony Bland. His parents, who visited him daily, were naturally hoping at first for signs of recovery, but the weeks and then the months went by – nothing. At last, they agreed with the doctors that it was futile to continue the tube-feeding that was maintaining his body; all he could do for himself was breathe. His doctor consulted the coroner before doing this and was told that he might be charged with murder or manslaughter. Dr Howe therefore applied to the Court for permission to stop treatment and so started Britain's first right-to-die case.

Evidence was given that the space once occupied by Tony's brain now contained a mass of fluid. He was in persistent vegetative state (PVS) and could not recover his ability to see, hear, taste, smell, feel, swallow or communicate in any way with the world around him. The judge ruled that it was lawful for all life-sustaining treatment to be discontinued. The case was sent to the Court of Appeal and then to the House of Lords, so that, in all, three senior judges and five law lords gave their separate arguments. One of their comments was that, had Tony ever indicated before the accident that he would not in these circumstances want life-sustaining treatment, such an indication would have settled the matter. Permission from the Court would not have been needed. As he had not so indicated, they had to consider his best interest. In the end they ruled that he had a right to have his bodily integrity respected – a principle called 'the right to privacy' in the United States – and this would not happen if he went on being physically cleaned and tube-fed, possibly for another

20 years or more. (The record is believed to be 36 years.)

Tony died peacefully nine days after the treatment was discontinued, and his parents could at last mourn the son they had, in effect, lost when he went off to the football match, almost four years before.

This case has made it easier for British doctors and the family together to decide to discontinue life-supporting treatment in cases of PVS. At first, inevitably, the family hopes for recovery, misled by the reflex actions that are governed by the brain stem. The patient may yawn, for example, or the fingers may grasp an object as a newborn baby's do. But researchers have investigated what happened a year later to patients who were diagnosed to be vegetative three months after their injury. Fifteen months after the accident, half were dead and one-third still vegetative. Only one in six had recovered any degree of consciousness, and all of them were severely disabled and totally dependent. The cases that are reported occasionally of people recovering fully from PVS are cases of mis-diagnosis, according to the *British Medical Journal* of February 1995.

In the United States the first right-to-die case occurred in 1976. The New Jersey Supreme Court ruled that Karen Quinlan's ventilator could be switched off. It was expected that she would be unable to breathe without the machine's help, but she was weaned from it gradually, and she survived for ten more years in PVS. There have been other cases since then, notably that of Nancy Cruzan, in 1990, when the United States Supreme Court sanctioned the removal of her feeding tube. It is interesting that the nurses caring for Nancy Cruzan said that if the feeding tube were to be removed in order to allow her to die, she should have been given a lethal injection. They did not regard death by starvation as humane.

Babies with a very poor prognosis of life form another category for whom agonizing decisions have to be made. The advance of modern techniques of life-preservation has meant the survival of many newborns whose quality of life is poor. The consultant paediatrician who battles to preserve the baby's life should perhaps think ahead to the probable outcome. Is the baby likely to be blind and deaf, incapable of independent movement and constantly crying in apparent distress? If so, is it right to inflict such an existence on the infant? And what about the parents and siblings, whose lives will be affected by caring for the new family member?

In Britain in 1996 the parents of two-year-old Thomas petitioned the High Court for permission to stop feeding him by stomach tube so that he would die. His brain damage was so profound that he was unable to hear, see or swallow and had little control over his limbs. He also suffered from epileptic fits. Thomas's life was one of manifest misery and had no chance of ever improving, but the loving care of his parents was obvious in a long, sensitively made programme, shown on British television early in 1996.

The arguments in Court in such a case were likely to be long and elaborate, but the basic opposition was between those, like Thomas's parents, who thought that a way must be found to end the child's suffering and those who claimed this was impossible. The spokesmen for the British Medical Association (BMA) and for the Roman Catholic church's law and medical ethics committee, approved of the doctors' decision not to give Thomas antibiotics if he developed pneumonia. To his parents this showed that the doctors thought his quality of life so poor that it should not be prolonged by medication if he developed a life-threatening illness. But they did not see why the infant had to go on choking – the mucus in his throat had to be sucked out frequently – and crying, while they continued with artificial feeding.

In the event, Thomas developed an infection and died before the case came to Court and however much one might wish to have a Court ruling that would spare similar infants from all that Thomas went through, one could only be thankful that this particular boy's suffering was over at last.

Those who argue against parents and doctors being allowed to agree to end a baby's life in these circumstances often resort to scaremongering. It will be a 'slippery slope', they say. If anyone is ever allowed to end a life because its quality is as poor as Thomas's was, they say, then 'why not draw up a list of people whose lives we think are not worth living?' The obvious answer to this is, who would think of doing such a thing?

The fact is that human thought and ingenuity have developed the medical means of preventing many deaths. In those rare cases where this turns out to be a bad thing, human thought and ingenuity will have to find a way of deciding to bring that thwarted death about. It will not do to shuffle away from that responsibility in the hope that a chance infection will make the decision for us. The medical and legal authorities have already faced this responsibility in some countries. In 1995 an international congress of ethics in medicine, meeting in New York, was told that in Norway very premature and very underweight babies are allowed to die.

'But a few of those babies might survive with a little bit of consciousness,' the American paediatrician reporting this had protested.

'Yes, we know that,' was the reply. 'It is part of the price we pay in return for not having preserved the lives of the majority who will not.'

Those who want to change the law to allow competent adults choice in dying do not suggest that the law needs to be changed in relation to PVS patients or grossly defective newborns. Joint decisions by doctors and families to discontinue inappropriate life-sustaining treatment are already very frequent. Codes of practice to guide them, including the proper recording of all these sad events, would surely be enough.

When it comes to adults who can decide for themselves, there are many who dislike the idea of ever being in a similar position to, say, Beatrice or Edith. They realize that in most countries doctors are not allowed to help them have the peaceful death they might crave. They begin to think about whether there will be anything they can do to help themselves in those or in different, but equally distressing, circumstances.

2

What can I do now to help myself have a good death?

◇

'Did you know that poor Doreen has passed away?'

'Oh, yes. What a blessing though. I do hope I don't linger the way she did.'

'Me too. What that family went through! Terrible, wasn't it?'

The hope expressed by these two friends – to be spared a long, slow death – crosses the minds of most people when someone they know endures one. Sometimes a vivid film evokes the same response. But most people do not realize that they can do better than hope; to some extent they can protect themselves from getting into that position.

The first thing to remember is that everyone has an absolute right to refuse medical treatment. Until recently in the United Kingdom, at any rate, it has been the custom by nearly all classes of society to accept a doctor's advice as though it could not be questioned. In fact the expression 'I'm under doctor's orders to do (or avoid) . . .' used to be heard frequently. Perhaps the speaker was quite happy to have the excuse to do (or avoid) whatever it was the doctor had advised, but no one questioned the implied authority of the doctor to tell a patient what to do or not to do, as the case might be. Sometimes it came in useful, as at a formal dinner in a London restaurant, which required gentlemen to wear a tie. 'Harry! However did you get past the doorman?' asked Norma, as Harry, late as usual, sat down in the empty chair next to her. His shirt was open at the neck, also as usual. None of those present had ever seen Harry in a tie.

He replied, 'I whispered "Doctor's orders, you know" as I passed him. No one ever questions that.'

But doctor's orders are *not* orders. What a doctor says is advice, which can be followed or not at the patient's discretion. Of course, most patients believe that the doctor will know what he or she is talking about and that the advice being given is correct according to the present state of medical knowledge. And most of the time they will be right. But most patients also assume that all doctors think alike and that they would get the same advice from any of them. Again, this may very well be true. But medical research advances at such a pace that it is sometimes a good idea to seek a second opinion. Few people want to waste a second doctor's time, and they feel it is rather rude to question their own doctor's advice. Nevertheless, even if one rarely does it, the possibility of getting different advice from another doctor should always be borne in mind.

Another closely connected point is that medical treatment must not be given without the patient's consent except in the most dire emergency, and not always even then.

> Jack was 78 years old and being nursed at home. He was suffering from arteriosclerosis, one of the many medical conditions associated with nicotine addiction. He had been a life-long smoker, and his arteries had become so narrowed that the circulation of his blood was very poor. He was confined to bed, had lost his appetite and did not even want to drink. But he was conscious, although not sleeping well. He was still a big, heavy man, and the nursing was strenuous. Even with visiting nurses, it was all getting too much for his 73-year-old wife.

The family doctor called in a consultant, who decreed that Jack must go into hospital in order to be properly cared for. When the ambulance arrived the next day Jack, who had for many years hated being away from home, even for a holiday, refused to go. His wishes, even when he shouted his protests and attempted to resist physically, were ignored. In hospital a drip was inserted in his arm to provide him with the water that he was unwilling to drink. This was done without his consent. His doctors would have had to claim it was an emergency to justify this treatment; otherwise it becomes a medical assault. None of the family was knowledgeable enough to realize this and to challenge the life-extending treatment.

Ten years later his only daughter listened to a hospice doctor read a paper about her latest piece of research. This described the discovery that a certain amount of dehydration was natural in those approaching death and caused no distress. In fact, giving water to overcome this was not to be recommended.

Jack had also been refusing food for several days before his admission to hospital. When his daughter timidly mentioned this to a senior nurse she was told, 'No, of course, we don't force anyone to eat. Our policy is of vigorous encouragement only.'

The sight of her father moving the unwanted food about his mouth in a valiant attempt to conform, moved her to tears.

There was worse to come, because the water and the small quantities of food he managed to swallow prolonged his life for a further seven weeks. By that time he was doubly incontinent, and his feet were becoming gangrenous. During the whole of that time he spoke very little. 'They'd be prosecuted if they kept a dog alive in this condition,' was one of the few remarks he did make.

If his wife or daughter, who visited him daily, attempted to hold his hand, he dug his nails into their

Longfoirt

hands as viciously as his little remaining strength allowed. He died apparently hating them for allowing him to be there, and they weren't there when he died, which happened at five o'clock one morning.

Afterwards, they reproached themselves for allowing him to be taken away from home and wondered why they had acted as they had. The answer was ignorance. They thought that if they defied the consultant's decision, he and the family doctor would wash their hands of them and say 'Look after him yourselves, then' and they knew they couldn't do that.

The crucial fact they did not know was that a doctor has a duty of care – that is, to keep the patient as comfortable and free from pain as possible, no matter how much other medical treatment is refused. For Jack, that knowledge came to them too late.

Carol was more fortunate in the last stages of her life. Twenty years ago, when she was in her early thirties, she developed breast cancer, and she was subjected to the last radical mastectomy that was performed in the British teaching hospital where she was treated. The procedure meant that the breast and some glands and muscular tissue were all removed, and the result was that the movement of her arm on that side was restricted. Carol's better fortune had not started yet, because the cancer had already spread before her mastectomy, and she had more operations. But she was kept informed of the treatment and gave her consent to all that was done. However, there came a day when further treatment was suggested by the consultant, and she said, 'No, thank you. I don't think I'll bother with that.'

The consultant was startled and told Carol's husband privately that it was very rare for a patient to refuse any medical treatment that was offered.

However, no one put pressure on Carol to change her mind. Perhaps they would have done so if the treatment had been likely to cure her, but by this time it was clear to everyone, including Carol, that no cure was possible. Even so, medical staff and family do sometimes urge patients to accept treatment whose only effect will be to make them die more slowly. Relatives may try to persuade the patient to accept such treatment because they cannot bear the prospect of parting with the dying one. Sometimes this feeling extends to overriding the patient's decision, but this husband recognized his wife's right to decide for herself.

A young journalist suffering from AIDS was keen to take part in a film, centring on his own case. In one of the last scenes he was in a hospice bed talking, with difficulty, to his widowed mother.

'I don't think I can take any more, Mum. I'm going to ask them now to help me end it all.'

'Oh, no!' she exclaimed. His only response was an infinitely weary sigh, so she continued, 'Go on then. I suppose you'll do as you like.'

'How can I when you take that attitude?' he answered.

That was the end of the scene. Viewers of the film were left to hope that the mother set aside her selfish wish to postpone for as long as possible having to face life without him. Perhaps she began to think of the long road of deterioration her son had travelled and to sympathize with his feeling that he had reached his limit. She might even have recognized that he was an adult and entitled to make his own decisions.

There could be many reasons medical staff try to persuade reluctant patients to accept more treatment, even though everyone knows it will not restore health. Some doctors and nurses see a patient's death as a defeat and want to postpone it for as long as possible. Some want to try newly discovered treatments for the possible benefit of future patients. For others, the mere fact that another treatment has been discovered is a reason for trying it, apparently without much consideration of the possible benefits and drawbacks to a particular patient. This last attitude is becoming less common.

Let us return to Carol. As well as recognizing his wife's autonomy, Carol's husband was a lecturer at the university to which the teaching hospital in which she was being treated was attached. This meant that he and Carol spoke to her doctors as colleagues – another distinct advantage when a lot depends on easy communication. Carol died at home, peacefully. She had talked openly about her cancer, and later about her impending death, to everyone, including her two daughters, who were in their early teens. They and their father survived their bereavement in much better shape than those families who are not able to talk freely. Remembering the past with their mother and thinking ahead together helped both girls and their father.

Carol and her husband had regularly attended the newly built church just across the road, and as part of her thinking ahead, she said, 'I'd like donations instead of flowers at my funeral. Send them to the Bell Fund. I've always been such a noisy person. It seems quite suitable.' Carol died with dignity, helping her family and then her church right up to the end, and beyond. The new bell has her name engraved round the rim, and although few people will ever see it, every Sunday someone probably thinks of her when they hear the bell.

Refusing further treatment when you are soon going to die, as Carol did, and as Jack would have liked to have done, is one thing. Refusing a blood transfusion that would restore you to normal health is another. One would think doctors would find an excuse to get round the patient's refusal, but this is not done unless parents are refusing on behalf of a child. Even that is a complicated legal process, which has become common only in recent years. Jehovah's Witnesses make this decision on the basis of a quotation from the Bible, and adult Jehovah's Witnesses continue to exercise their right of refusal. A few years ago the otherwise healthy mother of healthy, newborn twins, for example, bled to death by her own choice in an English hospital.

Most of us, who are not Jehovah's Witnesses, will want to refuse life-prolonging treatment only when we find that the quality of our life has dwindled to an unacceptable level and that there is no chance of an improvement. In those circumstances we will need to remember our legal rights. To be properly informed about our condition and the effects of any further treatment that is being offered is the first. The second is that any treatment given without our consent is an assault; we must make sure that we understand any consent form before we sign it. Then there is our basic right to refuse treatment. And lastly, we have a right to comfort care after we have refused treatment directed at extending our lives (or postponing our deaths, depending on your point of view).

As long as we are conscious and our minds remain clear, as long as we still have the vigour to argue if need be and, preferably, as long as we have a close relative who thoroughly knows our wishes and is prepared to help us, all should be well. We ought to be allowed to die in peace if that is what we want. But it is a long list of 'ifs', and sadly it can all go very wrong, as the following two cases show.

'She was my friend from school days together in Berlin. We both got out of Nazi Germany in time and have lived in Oxford ever since.' Eva, aged 87, was speaking of her friend who had had a massive stroke. At the hospital a feeding tube had been inserted up this old lady's nose, despite the protests of her daughter and her old friend. 'We both knew she wouldn't have wanted that.

Fortunately she died a few days later anyway. Why wouldn't they listen to us, who knew her wishes?'

A few years before, a teacher had described visiting a colleague in hospital. 'We weren't close friends, but I knew she hadn't any surviving relatives so I went to see her one day. I was shocked to see how ill she looked and to see her left leg had been amputated. She wasn't very keen on talking about it, but I got the impression that she hadn't felt there was any choice in the matter. I didn't manage to get there very frequently, but she didn't re-cover enough to leave hospital. It was months later that one of the doctors took me on one side and said, "Her other leg needs amputating now, but we've decided not to do it. We'll just let nature take its course." I didn't say anything, but it wasn't clear to me that my colleague had wanted the first amputation. And the way he put it, it didn't sound as though she was the one deciding about the second one either.'

So another good idea is to talk to your family doctor about how you feel. In the absence of close relatives and/or friends willing and able to put your point of view, a sympathetic doctor can be a tower of strength.

Better still, however, is to write down what we would want, just in case we cannot speak up for ourselves to refuse un-wanted treatment, when, or if, such a time ever comes. The first person to do this was a Chicago lawyer, Luis Kutner, in 1969. He called the document he produced for this purpose a 'living will'. The enthusiastic use of every new medical dis-covery has always been more common in the United States than anywhere else, so American citizens stood in the most need of protecting themselves from being kept alive in-definitely. It was no wonder that the American Right-to-die Society took up the idea immediately and issued living wills to its members.

In California in 1976 a state law was passed recognizing

living wills, and other states followed. It now applies in 47 states. Indeed, in 1990 a federal law (applying to every state) obliged all hospitals that receive government money to discuss with patients what their wishes would be about the use of life-prolonging measures if they were to reach a terminal condition.

In 1969 there were very few societies in the rest of the world campaigning for patient choice in dying. One of them, the British Voluntary Euthanasia Society, immediately saw the usefulness of having such a document but gave it another name, the advance directive. Its purpose is exactly the same as its American equivalent, the living will.

Eva died a few years after her friend, whose wish not to have artificial feeding had been disregarded. Eva did not have a stroke but died peacefully at home after a short illness, so the question of putting her on machines to stop her dying did not arise. But if it had done, her relatives would have been in a stronger position to insist on her wishes being respected because they had a copy of her advance directive (see example on pages 38–40). Eva had taken this form to her doctor many years before her death and asked him to be the first witness. This meant that no hospital doctor, wanting to give her tube-feeding after a stroke, could suggest that she had not really understood what she was signing.

Sometimes family doctors have refused to sign an advance directive. This may have been because the form came from the Voluntary Euthanasia Society and they assumed, without reading it, that it asked for actual euthanasia – that is, a lethal injection. No document that asked a doctor to commit a crime could possibly be legal, but presumably a doctor who refuses to accept an advance directive has not even realized that. One woman whose family doctor reacted like this went to the minister of her church for help. The minister took time to read the form, said how much she agreed with it, and accompanied the woman on another visit to the doctor. This time the advance directive was read attentively, signed and put in the patient's notes.

TO MY FAMILY, PHYSICIAN AND ALL OTHER PERSONS CONCERNED THIS DIRECTIVE is made by me .... at a time when I am of sound mind and after careful consideration.

I DECLARE that if at any time the following circumstances exist, namely:

1. I suffer from one or more of the conditions mentioned in the schedule; and
2. I have become unable to participate effectively in decisions about my medical care; and
3. two independent physicians (one a consultant) are of the opinion that I am unlikely to recover from illness or impairment involving severe distress or incapacity for rational existence,

THEN AND IN THOSE CIRCUMSTANCES my directions are as follows:

1. that I am not to be subjected to any medical intervention or treatment aimed at prolonging or sustaining my life;
2. that any distressing symptoms (including any caused by lack of food or fluid) are to be fully controlled by appropriate analgesic or other treatment, even though that treatment may shorten my life.

I consent to anything proposed to be done or omitted in compliance with the directions expressed above and absolve my medical attendants from any civil liability arising out of such acts or omissions.

I wish it to be understood that I fear degeneration and indignity far more than I fear death. I ask my medical attendants to bear this statement in mind when considering what my intentions would be in any uncertain situation.

I RESERVE the right to revoke this DIRECTIVE at any time, but unless I do so it should be taken to represent my continuing directions.

SCHEDULE

A Advanced malignant disease (cancer)

B Severe immune deficiency (AIDS)

C Advanced degenerative disease of the nervous system (MS or MND)

D Severe and lasting brain damage due to injury, stroke, disease or other cause

E Senile or pre-senile dementia, whether Alzheimer's, multi-infarct or other

F Any other condition of comparable gravity

*I nominate (name in capitals)...

of (address) ....

....

(tel. no.) ....

as a person to be consulted by my medical attendants when considering what my intentions would be in any uncertain situation.

*Delete if not applicable

My general practitioner is (name of doctor)...........................

of (address)..

(tel. no.)..

*Before signing this directive I talked it over with my doctor.

*Delete if not applicable

Signed..

Date..

WE TESTIFY that the maker of this Directive signed it in our presence, and made it clear that he/she understood what it meant. We do not know of any pressure being brought on him/her to make such a directive and we believe it was made by his/her own wish. So far as we are aware we do not stand to gain from his/her will.

Witnessed by:

Signature............................	Signature............................
Name...................................	Name...................................
Address..............................	Address..............................
....	....
....	....

This Directive was reviewed and confirmed by me on the following dates (sign your name each time you enter a date).

Even with the help of an advance directive (sometimes called an 'advance statement') the decisions to be made by doctors and family, however well they know the patient's views and however much they sympathize, are still by no means straightforward. This is chiefly because it is so difficult to judge the likely outcome.

'I've just been to a "Welcome Home!" party for one of my patients. The intensive care consultant and her parents and I were on the verge of switching off all the machines. Then we decided we'd wait just another 24 hours.' The rest of the group stared at the doctor who had just told them this, with a mixture of awe, amazement and a tinge of hostility. They had met to discuss forgoing life-prolonging treatment, and most of them were in favour of it. At last one of them said: 'She must be very happy.'

'No, she isn't,' was the unexpected reply. 'She's very angry, especially with me. She'll never walk again and she's handicapped in other ways. She says she wishes we'd switched the machines off.' The woman probably accepted her diminished life as time went by, but perhaps she never did. Even with hindsight, it is not easy to know whether the doctors and relatives made the best decision. At the time it is even harder to decide what to do.

Nevertheless, advance directives are a great help to both doctors and the family. For example, the doctors do not have to worry about the family later regretting the decision and blaming the doctors for it. In Britain, unlike the United States, it has been rare for patients to sue their doctors or even to make a formal complaint, but the numbers of complaints are steadily increasing, and the possibility of legal action is something that doctors have to be aware of. Although the relatives may have agreed at the time that it was best to stop all the strenuous efforts to maintain the life, a feeling of guilt, of not having done enough for the dead person, is almost universal in the early stages of bereavement. Shifting that burden by blaming the doctor for the decision is very easy – somewhat on the following lines.

'I didn't really think we should have turned off the ventilator. Maybe she would have started breathing on her own again if we'd waited a bit longer.'

'Well, why didn't you say so? I wanted to wait, really.'

'It was that doctor. Rushing us into it like that. I've a good mind to complain to the hospital about it.'

There cannot be any of that sort of thing with an advance directive. It says 'I absolve my medical attendants from blame' (although in more legally explicit words), and feeling guilty about having done it makes even less sense when the relatives are merely abiding by the patient's own wishes.

Another benefit is where there is conflict between relatives. Pauline was dying in great distress, and her two adult children sympathized with her wish that it could all be over. Their fairly newly acquired step-father, however, had not come to terms with the fact that his wife was dying and he was urging the doctors to do all they could to prolong her life. It was not at all obvious to the doctors who took priority. An advance directive would have been a great help to everyone, for Pauline could have written on her advance directive the name of the relative she wished to speak on her behalf. The most common expression for giving another person the right to speak or vote on your behalf is 'appointing a proxy', or it can be called giving that person an 'enduring power of attorney'. This already happens when someone becomes incapable through ill-health of managing their own affairs. But the person who holds that power of attorney is not entitled to make decisions about health care.

So far, the countries that have recognized advance directives (living wills) are the United States, Canada, some Australian states and Denmark. In Britain it is likely that there will soon be legislation 'extending the right to refuse treatment into a time of future incapacity', as one judge has put it. This is because the Law Commission and the British Medical Association (BMA) are both supporting it. The BMA has changed its attitude since 1988. Its handbook *Euthanasia* (1988) says: ' . . . a judicious medical paternalism may well be the best and most realistic way to achieve a good outcome. . . . But a certified and settled wish by a patient should always be treated with the utmost respect.' This seems to accord with the response of an intensive care consultant during a television discussion programme. When asked if he paid any attention to an advance directive he replied: 'Yes, provided it fits in with what I've already decided to do.'

By 1995 the BMA had so far changed its attitude as to trigger a row at the Annual General Meeting of the World Medical Association by insisting that severely ill unconscious patients who had left clear instructions that they did not want to be revived should be allowed to die. The international declaration on the rights of patients includes a statement that: 'medical consent to treatment should be presumed if the patient is unconscious and unable to give consent . . . unless it is obvious and beyond any doubt on the basis of the patient's previous firm expression that he/she would refuse consent to intervention in that situation.' So far so good, but then it adds: 'However, physicians should always try to save the life of a patient unconscious due to a suicide attempt.'

The BMA representative objected to the 'always'. In other words, he was recognizing that suicide may be a rational course of action for someone who is incurably ill and unable to get help to die. Most countries voted against the BMA, saying that its position was the first step towards euthanasia, a charge that its chairman vigorously denied.

The code is not binding on medical associations and has no force of law. But the BMA stance means that no British doctor can claim to be ethically in line with his colleagues if he or she insists that a doctor's duty is always to preserve life.

The fact that Parliament has not yet passed a law about advance directives in Britain does not mean they can be ignored by doctors. This is because of case law. In 1994 a schizophrenic patient decided he would rather die with two legs than live with one, and he applied to the High Court for an injunction to prevent doctors amputating his gangrenous leg, if he became incapable of forbidding it. This patient had had experience during his illness of being at times incapable of expressing himself rationally. The judge, who travelled to the hospital to talk to him, was satisfied that he understood the medical information he had been given and was capable of making up his own mind, and he ruled that the man's current refusal of treatment must extend into a future time of possible incapacity.

Unless Parliament passed a law contradicting this judge's ruling, it could be used in any future cases in which a doctor ignored an advance directive. Since this is most unlikely, is it really necessary for there to be a law recognizing advance directives? Well, it isn't necessary to make them legally binding on doctors – it's more a case of dotting the i's and crossing the t's. For example, the intensive care doctor who said he ignored an advance directive if he did not agree with what it said was speaking after this legal case, but he seemed unaware of the implications of the judge's decision. The publicity surrounding the passage of the Bill through Parliament would help to dispel that ignorance, and there might also be a section requiring medical education on the subject, of the kind that was included in the United States Federal Law on Patient Self-Determination.

Family doctors may be required to take proper care of their copy of a patient's advance directive and see that it goes to hospital with them. The Danish law requires that the names of all those who have completed this document are held centrally, so that doctors having to make tricky decisions about an unconscious patient can quickly check whether they have made an advance directive. In the present state of computerized information, and in a country with a small population, that is a feasible proposition. In any case proper records will probably have to be kept of their use when advance directives are controlled by statute law. A separate question is whether the new law will include giving the patient the power to appoint an attorney to make decisions on health care.

All in all, we may conclude that it is a good idea to get an advance directive form, complete it (preferably with your doctor's cooperation) and give a copy to the friend or relative most likely to be speaking for you. If you know that some members of your family are likely to be more sympathetic to your wishes than others, you will be able to name the person you would prefer to speak on your behalf.

Under those circumstances it is, for example, most unlikely that you would have a feeding tube inserted into your stomach after a severe stroke, as happened to an 82-year-old lady, much against the wishes of her husband who knew she wouldn't want it, but had no evidence of her wishes. And if it were done, your relatives would be able to sue the doctors who did it. This is important, because the possibility will discourage a doctor who thinks he or she knows better than you do what is in your best interest.

In the present state of the law in almost all countries, however, being allowed to die is the limit of the help to a dignified death we can receive. This is usually called passive euthanasia to distinguish it from active euthanasia, in which drugs are given so that death follows within hours. Patients who depend on a machine to keep them alive can ask for the machine to be switched off, and they, too, will die within a short time. Kidney dialysis patients sometimes decide they have had enough of the burdensome treatment and give it up. Since dying from kidney failure can be very painful and distressing, they are given sedative drugs. These are the same drugs that are used in hospices for those patients whose pain cannot be controlled by any other means.

Nowadays the young woman who had spent her life in an iron lung would probably be allowed to discontinue its use and to be given those drugs. She wrote many years ago to the Voluntary Euthanasia Society as follows:

> *I had polio when I was seven and have spent 25 years in an iron lung at home. My parents have looked after me. I have always said I would never want to go on like this in an institution. Now my father has a bad heart and my mother can't look after both of us, so I have decided this has gone on long enough.*
>
> *I can manage outside the machine for a very short period (while I am cleaned up), so I have asked them to leave me outside. But I couldn't bear the feeling of suffocation and I had to ask to be put back.*
>
> *I've tried being put near an open window in the hope that I'll get pneumonia, but that hasn't worked. Please help me.*

The Society could not help her, but someone should have been able to talk to her and to find out if there really was so little for her to enjoy in life that she preferred to be dead. Perhaps a place at an institution she would find acceptable could have been found. And if all else failed she should have been allowed to die, like those refusing further dialysis.

Iron lungs have been replaced by portable ventilators, which allow the user a much better quality of life. At the same time, the legal and medical attitudes to the refusal of medical treatment have softened in most advanced industrial countries. Recently a young man died in the special spinal unit of the hospital in Salisbury, England. He had spent 18 months on a ventilator after breaking his neck in an accident and becoming completely paralysed. The coroner recorded a verdict that he died as a result of a decision not to take insulin. His father said: 'David had our complete respect. He could make decisions, there was nothing else he could do.'

Because he was diabetic, David did not even have to ask someone else to switch off the ventilator.

Few of us are actually dependent on life-supporting machinery or on insulin when we reach the stage of judging that our life is no longer worth living so there is nothing to be switched off and no insulin to be refused. DNR (do not resuscitate) orders can be made, and provided that all the relevant medical staff know about them, you may be allowed to die in peace next time your nearly worn-out heart stops beating, but that may not be for weeks, or even months. Or it may be decided that, if you develop pneumonia, you will not be given antibiotics. Again, however, the pneumonia that the doctors expect to allow you to die from, without attempting to cure it, may not develop for weeks. Or you may get pneumonia and recover from it spontaneously, so that in the end, long after the decision not to treat your pneumonia, you die of something else. It is a bleak prospect.

Many potential patients (including those who are at present doctors) feel it is a hypocritical state of affairs. The decision not to treat used to be called TLC (tender loving care), meaning 'give nursing care only, do not give drugs that would cure any infection that develops'. There are no rules about involving the patient, if he or she is still capable, or the concerned relatives in this decision, by the way. Surely there should be. Even assuming that the doctors and nursing team have got it right and that both the patient and relatives are in accord, what this decision amounts to is nothing more than 'the only remaining good thing that can happen to this patient is to die'. It is a human decision for death, and at that stage standing back and allowing 'God' or 'Nature' or a microbe or a virus to take charge strikes many as an evasion of a human responsibility.

To be able to get positive medical help to die without involving in a criminal act the doctor who does it means changing the law. In some countries this process is already on its way. Elsewhere and in the meantime, many of us are having to plan to act for ourselves. It isn't what we would choose, but the alternative – of going on deteriorating past the point at which we consider life worth living – is worse.

3
What happens when someone finds their life has no remaining quality?

◇

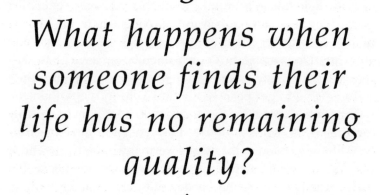

It was such a relief when I finally decided that living in such constant pain gave me a moral right to commit suicide. I can only remember a few very short periods in my life when I was suddenly and wonderfully conscious of being totally pain-free.

Marjorie was brought up as a Roman Catholic and therefore to believe that suicide is a mortal sin and anyone guilty of it would go to Hell. She has also suffered throughout her life from rheumatoid arthritis and osteoarthritis. She went on:

As soon as I decided that I could escape from it if I found life unbearable I immediately thought that I would have a duty to make as good a thing as possible of my life until I reached that point. And things have got better and better since I started thinking in that more positive way. I still keep a balance sheet though, and when it tips too far towards the unpleasantness getting the upper hand, I intend to take action.

Of course, I would much prefer to have my doctor there to help me. I don't really want to die alone, and I'm afraid of not succeeding in my attempt. It isn't so easy to commit suicide as some people seem to think.

In the many years since Marjorie made her momentous decision, research into pain control has advanced a great deal. She has to take a bewildering variety of pills, and the side-effects of some of them are not pleasant. But, with crutches, she can walk and on the days when she feels equal to making the effort of getting to the swimming pool, she can swim. 'That's the only place where I feel like a normal person,' she says.

Suicide is no longer a crime in most countries. In a few it never was. Many young people are incredulous when they learn that suicide was a crime in England and Wales until 1961. 'How could you ever prosecute someone who is dead?' they say. And, of course, that was never possible, but at one time a suicide's property was confiscated by the Crown, and until 1961 failed suicides were liable to be charged with the attempted crime as soon as they recovered.

In the same countries, the Church of England, to which the majority of the population nominally belong, forbade the burial of a suicide in hallowed ground. The body was frequently buried at a crossroads, and often a stake was driven through the grave. Actually the description says with a stake 'through the heart', so presumably the body was in a shroud rather than a coffin. The last such burial in Britain was in 1823 at Hobart Place, within a stone's throw of Buckingham Palace. It is no wonder that many people, especially older ones, still associate suicide with shame and disgrace. It takes a lot of suffering to make anyone even contemplate it.

The very word 'suicide' implies a crime, evoking the image of self-murder. It is interesting that the Dutch can distinguish between ending one's life because of something that would most probably cure itself in time, and the rational decision that results from recognizing an incurable condition that can only get worse. The first they call *zeldmoord* or self-murder, and the second *zelfdoding* or self-deathing.

Edith, whom we met earlier, discarded the idea of ending her own life, but did not go into details about her reasons. The feeling that it would be a disgraceful way to die must, to a woman of her generation, have played a part in her thinking. She would not have wanted her memory to be tainted by it, and she would not have wanted her daughter to be associated with anything so unpleasant.

If we think about Edith's decision more carefully, we will realize that there was probably another big difficulty behind it: how was she to do it? The suicides that had happened in the neighbourhoods where she had lived would have been spoken of in hushed tones as 'and he was hanging from the banisters when she got home' or 'she kept on saying she was going to put her head in the gas oven, and in the end she did'. Other methods of ending her life would not have occurred to her. She knew she was too frail to hang herself and that natural gas, unlike the old coal gas, is not poisonous enough to be effective. Knowing that her doctor would not help her and unwilling to involve her daughter in anything illegal, she gave up the idea. The daughter would have been guilty of 'aiding, abetting, counselling or procuring a suicide' and, if convicted, could have been sentenced to 14 years' imprisonment. This is one of the rare examples of it being illegal to help someone to perform a legal act.

It was with the predicament of people like Marjorie and Edith in mind that in 1980 the Voluntary Euthanasia Society decided to publish a handbook called *A Guide to Self-deliverance* (self-deliverance being as near as it could get to self-deathing). The preface was written by Arthur Koestler, and it included a lot of advice to those intending using it about checking carefully that there really was no way of making life acceptable again rather than ending it all. By this time the Society had been in existence for 45 years and had made several attempts to get Parliament to change the law, but without success. Despite the fact that the handbook was available only to Society members of long-standing, there was such a flurry of legal proceedings that the VES reluctantly stopped issuing it. The High Court judge who ruled that legal action *might* be taken against the Society for aiding and abetting if the

handbook were found in the possession of a suicide, commented favourably on the quality of its contents. The High
Court ruling also said that if the handbook were published for
general sale there could be no legal objection. No one would
be entitled to assume that a purchaser intended to act on the
information in it, but anyone who bought it from a voluntary
euthanasia organization might be reasonably supposed to
have the idea of committing suicide in mind.

The Scottish members of the VES formed a separate Society,
VESS, and issued a handbook of its own, with substantially
similar advice. The argument was that, since suicide had never
been a crime in Scotland, the 1961 Suicide Act could not apply
there. There have been no prosecutions, and VESS continues to
up-date and issue the handbook to its members.

Meantime, in the United States a book called *Let Me Die
Before I Wake* had been published and was on open sale there.
It was followed a few years later by *Final Exit*. This book shot
to the top of the best-seller list, to the considerable astonish-
ment of its author, Derek Humphry. It has been translated into
14 languages and is available in bookshops throughout the
English-speaking world.

All these books give similar advice. If you have reached the
point where your quality of life is quite unacceptable, be sure
you talk about your decision to end your life, if possible, to
your close family and your doctor. Think carefully about any
suggested further treatments for your condition. Do not use
violent methods – for example, throwing yourself under a
train or off a tall building or cutting your wrists. There are
really only two safe ways of achieving your aim and even then
you must take precautions against failure. In either case, a
written message to whoever finds you is a good idea, if you
can manage it.

Access to a car provides many suicides with a painless
death. A hose from the exhaust pipe through a slightly opened
window will fill the car with toxic fumes, as long as the engine
is left running. Being found prematurely is the commonest

reason for this method not to be successful.

Although non-drivers are becoming increasingly rare, not everyone has unquestioned access to a car. In addition, many people, perhaps most, who are incurably ill and fully intend to evade the closing stages of their illness nevertheless postpone action as long as they are finding anything to enjoy in life. This means that they are often physically unable to use car exhaust fumes, as described above. For them the means of escape must be primarily drugs.

The main problems with this course are knowing which drugs will be painlessly effective and then getting hold of them. Those, especially doctors, who have professional access to that knowledge and of the actual drugs that will end their life have a higher rate of suicide (and a lower rate of attempted but failed suicide) than the general population. A third difficulty is that it takes much longer for most drugs to take effect if they are swallowed and have to work their way through the digestive system, than if they are injected. For all these reasons, one reads in many accounts of suicides that the body was found with a plastic bag over the head.

In 1993 the *Guardian* newspaper reported the suicide of Lady Eva Green. She was found with a plastic bag over her head tied with a knotted length of elastic. The doctor who carried out the post-mortem said she had taken four to five times the therapeutic level of Temazepam, used to reduce anxiety and help sleep, although the level was not enough to kill her. He supported the possible scenario put forward by the coroner that she would have felt drowsy and at that point placed the bag over her head. He said: 'Death is remarkably rapid with this method, with no signs of asphyxia.'

An American doctor, the chief medical examiner for the state of Connecticut, supports this view from his wide experience of seeing the bodies of such suicides. Their faces are neither blue nor swollen. He is quoted as saying: 'They just look ordinary – but dead.' Death comes about because the oxygen in the air is gradually used up and, lacking oxygen, a peaceful death follows. There have been reports of would-be suicides pulling the plastic bag off while they were still alert enough to do so. It is not known whether this was because the plastic bag was too small, so the oxygen got used up before they were fully asleep, or whether they were not as fully committed to the intention of committing suicide as they had thought they were.

Of course, dying in this way is not to be compared with voluntary euthanasia. For one thing, it must take place in solitude, because anyone present is likely to be charged with aiding and abetting a suicide.

Molly had agreed to stay with a neighbour who had decided to take her own life. Pearl, aged 84, had been an orphan who had never married, so she was entirely without family. She had led a satisfying life, earning her own living at a job she enjoyed and retiring on a pension that was adequate. But she was now blind and going deaf. Going on would involve losing her independence and she had decided otherwise. Adjusting the plastic bag was difficult, and Molly helped her to get comfortable with it in place. She held Pearl's hand until she realized it was growing cold, then she removed the bag, fluffed up the disarranged hair and left. There was no inquest. The natural death of such a frail old lady surprised no one. Molly had found the whole experience emotionally draining, although she was sure she had done the right thing in helping Pearl to die in the manner and at the time of her own choice.

A few weeks later she talked about what had happened to someone she regarded as a friend. This person reported what she had heard to the police, Molly was found guilty of aiding and abetting a suicide and sentenced to one year's imprisonment.

Cooperating with a suicidal person is dangerous, a fact that

was in the mind of an older woman when the following conversation took place. One of her close friends had just taken
her own life. 'You wouldn't do a silly thing like that, would
you?' asked her daughter.

'No, I wouldn't,' replied her mother. 'She didn't even wait
for the tests to know whether her breast cancer had spread or
not, she just thought it had. If mine flares up again I'll be
certain before I take action. And she didn't talk to her children
about her plans. I wouldn't do that either.'

After a pause, thinking of her dead friend, also a widow
and also, up to that point, emotionally close to her adult
children, she added sadly, 'Of course, none of you could be
there in case you were charged with aiding and abetting me.'

The daughter, speaking quietly but firmly, said, 'That's a
decision you might leave to us.' Both of them were well aware
of what had happened to Molly.

The mother apologized for going on behaving as though
her two sons and two daughters, ranging in age from 30 to 40,
were still not old enough to decide momentous things for
themselves. If they decided that staying with their mother was
more important than avoiding the risk of a criminal charge,
they clearly had the right to do so, but the thought of what
might happen to them was going to add one more difficulty to
ending her own life, if it ever became necessary.

In 1993 a family friend took a bottle of paracetamol into
hospital and gave them to a patient there, at the patient's request. Joyce had suffered from multiple sclerosis for 13 years,
was in a wheelchair and fed through tubes. She died from an
overdose of the tablets, and the friend was charged with aiding and abetting her suicide. The judge held that the friend
had 'only provided her with an option of taking her own life',
and the case was dismissed.

Some incurably ill people who find their quality of life unacceptable manage to commit suicide without any help. One
of these was the world-famous child psychologist, Bruno
Bettelheim. His death was the more remarkable because he

was in hospital at the time and was 82 years old. The obituary writers glossed over the manner of his death, or related it to his experience of a Nazi concentration camp 50 years earlier. He had been held there briefly before the war, while the camps still bore some resemblance to ordinary detention centres. He was released and allowed to leave Germany in response to international pressure at governmental level, the same thing that had happened to Sigmund Freud, except that Freud came to England and Bettelheim to the United States.

When he decided to end his life, Bettelheim had been a widower for three years and found it sad to be without his life-long companion. He had had two strokes, which left him considerably incapacitated, and he dreaded another. He could no longer swallow solid food. One biographer said that he wrote to Hemlock, the biggest American right-to-die society: 'He always believed in getting the best possible advice.'

Freud, too, organized his own death. He was helped to die by his doctor when the cancer of the mouth that he had endured so stoically for 23 years finally got the better of him. In 1990 Jaap van Velsen, a distinguished social anthropologist, ended his own life when his multiple sclerosis finally became too disabling. And in 1994 a French philosopher, Sarah Kofman, took her own life at the age of 60 after years of serious illness. The American physicist and Nobel prize-winner, Percy Bridgman, shot himself in 1961 at the age of 79. He was in the final stages of cancer. In conversation not long before this he told a colleague: 'When the ultimate end is as inevitable as mine appears to be, the individual has a right to ask his doctor to end it for him.' And in his suicide note he wrote: 'It is not decent for Society to make a man do this to himself. Probably this is the last day I will be able to manage it.'

Rational suicide – that is, choosing to die when finally weary of enduring an incurable illness – is by no means confined to famous and eminent people. Philip was a pathologist who hanged himself. The post-mortem revealed that he had cancer of the lungs, liver, spine and ribs. The coroner said that he had probably realized from his symptoms what he was suffering from and 'what a grim and harrowing future lay ahead'.

Matthew, who had been a keen squash player but was in a wheelchair because of his multiple sclerosis, attempted suicide unsuccessfully the first time. Three years later he succeeded. An 82-year-old who dreaded having to go into a residential home had two unsuccessful attempts before dying of his deliberate overdose. Walter's heart was in poor condition and his eyesight was failing.

Mrs Fulton's mode of death was by car exhaust fumes. She had had a slight stroke two years earlier and had said repeatedly that she did not intend to go on living after her husband's expected death. She promised her daughter she would wait for three months. And she did. She was 78 years old. Mary was 85 when she died of an overdose of sleeping tablets. She had been having severe back pain for a long time.

Perhaps these people would not have chosen to die with help from their own doctor, in their own bed, possibly with a loved relative or friend to hold their hand. Perhaps they would still have chosen their lonely, uncertain deaths. But it does not seem likely. As matters stand, their choice was between going on, which they were finding unendurable, or dying as they did.

Traditionally, old people whose health has failed and who now only want to die have 'turned their face to the wall' and refused all further nourishment. Some doctors speak of this as though it were a painless and comparatively easy way to die. Peter had spoken for many years, to his friends and in television programmes, of his wish to have voluntary euthanasia when his multiple sclerosis had progressed to the point where he preferred to die. But by the time that point came, the law still did not allow it and he could do nothing positive about it by himself. He said: 'My mind has become sharper than ever, but my body has been reduced to a useless shell. I am trapped.' He decided to escape by starvation, but he experienced such distressing symptoms that he was driven to relieve them by taking some light nourishment. It took seven weeks for him to die.

The previous summer Harriet had been more fortunate. She was in her early eighties, a fit, busy woman who had long since learned to live alone after her husband's death. Her children were close enough, emotionally and physically, to have heard her say a few times that she would definitely not want to be kept alive in a condition of dependence. She had a severe stroke but recovered her speech after a few days. 'I'll make a real effort with the rehabilitation programme for six months,' she told Paul, the son who later told her story on a radio programme, 'and then we'll see.' At the end of that time she judged that not much more progress was likely, and she asked her doctors to end her life. Apparently neither she nor her adult children had realized that this was illegal and that it was highly unlikely that she would find a doctor to do as she asked. And she didn't.

'Very well,' she said, 'I'll starve myself.' She discharged herself from hospital. That weekend the family and a few close friends had a goodbye gathering, and on the Monday she stayed in bed. Paul was the one who was able to take the most time off work to be with her, though the other three all took turns. It was a good family. The family doctor called every day, prescribing drugs that would ease any discomforts and advising them about the nursing care. The chief of these is making sure that the mouth does not become dry. At first she talked occasionally, and almost to the end she managed a serene smile.

'How long did it take?' someone on the radio panel asked.

'Twelve days.'

It was better than seven weeks, but it must have seemed like eternity, even so, to those watchers, especially Paul. 'Yes, it did,' he said. 'But it was all we could do. Otherwise we might have been found guilty of aiding and abetting her suicide.

When Christine decided to join the Voluntary Euthanasia Society she wrote:

> *My son, after much mental and physical suffering with multiple sclerosis, took his own life by carbon monoxide poisoning in his car. The coroner said, 'He was a brave young man.' The doctor said to us privately that he had done the brave and sensible thing, as his condition was inexorably deteriorating. There was a pamphlet about your Society among the papers he left, so I feel that by joining I am doing as he would wish.*

All these deaths were rational suicides. In the judgement of the person concerned there was no chance of recovering a state of health good enough to make a life worth living. Sadly, the overwhelming number of suicides are of someone, often young, whose physical health is normal but who, as the inquest verdict goes, 'took his life while the balance of his mind was disturbed'. These are irrational suicides.

It is estimated that two-thirds of British suicides are by people known to have had psychiatric illness. A study reported in *The Lancet* in 1993 showed that in the first month after discharge following a short stay in a psychiatric hospital, men were 213 times, and women 134 times, more likely to kill themselves than the population as a whole. The research was carried out in Oxford and covered 14,240 patients discharged from psychiatric hospitals between the mid-1970s and 1987. Providing good care at this stage, and indeed for all those suffering from depression, is of prime importance if they are to regain their capacity for enjoying life.

Making it legal for a doctor to help an incurably ill person to die at that person's long-considered and testified request would not allow help to suicidal depressives who were physically well. The medical profession would not classify mental illness as incurable.

Ignoring the distinction between rational suicides – that is, those people who would qualify for voluntary euthanasia if it were legally available – and the irrational suicides of the mentally ill makes it difficult to estimate how many rational suicides there are, but even if the numbers are small, we cannot ignore their plight unless we are callous about unnecessary human suffering.

James was a young man, permanently confined to a wheelchair following a motorcycle accident. He had a specially adapted bungalow, and he had enough movement in one hand to operate his wheelchair himself. He described his situation at the first conference of the World Federation of Right-to-die Societies, although he spoke of what he intended to do about it only to one close friend. One day he drove his chair towards the nearby river, but its motor stalled on the rough grass of the river bank. 'I'll have to wait a bit now,' he said. 'They'll be watching me.'

Next time he was successful. He managed to set fire to his bungalow and perished in the flames.

Another young man, Christopher, had been a policeman until an armed robber's bullet lodged in his spine and condemned him too to a chair-bound life. He tried it for six months, then he shot himself.

As observers we much prefer to read about Stephen Hawkings and his achievements in theoretical physics, despite the fact that motor neurone disease (MND) has reduced him to a far worse state of physical incapacity than either James or Christopher. But they did not have the resources of his exceptional intellect to fall back on, and they were the only ones in a position to judge what their present and future looked like to *them*. Their fate seems a cruel one, and to find a way to help them make their final choice and, if their decision was settled, let them have a more merciful death, is surely as much our duty as citizens as it is to rehabilitate the sufferers from depression. In the play and film *Whose Life Is It, Anyway?* the hero is finally allowed to refuse the medical care that is keeping him alive as a quadriplegic (paralysed from the neck down). Its author, Brian Clark, relates that on publicity tours he has watched the film in countries where audience behaviour is less sophisticated than in the United States and western Europe, and a great cheer always goes up when the judge gives the hero permission to choose to die.

In 1985 a real-life 33-year-old American man in the same situation was also allowed by a judge to have his life-supporting medical treatment withdrawn.

Henry was near the end of his lifespan, well into his eighties and dying of cancer. His son lived in a college of Oxford University and it was there, during a visit to his son, that Henry was found dead. He had cut his wrists. This was one of the methods of suicide used by eminent Roman citizens in classical times, when, in what were regarded as appropriate circumstances, suicide was an honourable way to die. Considering Henry's age and surroundings, it was possibly a background of a classical education that made him choose such a death.

Martha lived in Australia. She suffered from a rare and incurable condition, which meant that she was subject to frequent haemorrhaging 'usually from the nose'. This happened with no warning and the quantities of blood she lost were frighteningly large. All that medical science could offer her were regular blood tests and then blood transfusions when she became anaemic enough to make that necessary. When she was 63, Martha decided this did not add up to a life worth living. She had seen one of the spokesmen for legalizing voluntary euthanasia talking about it on television, and she wrote, asking for help.

Hundreds of miles away, Frances wrote back, explaining that no one could legally help her, but suggesting Martha talk to her doctor, her family, other helping agencies. Nothing seemed to come of that, but a later letter said: 'I am selling my house and buying a flat in a high-rise block. Do you think the eleventh floor will be high enough?'

There was a pause of some months in the correspondence. In the midst of her busy professional life, her family concerns and her spare-time campaigning for legal reform to the law on voluntary euthanasia, Frances would think of Martha, hopefully. Perhaps her doctors had found a way of relieving her distressing condition, for every day, after all, medical science is coming up with new ways of coping with the various diseases that afflict mankind, or perhaps Martha had found some brave soul who was willing, despite the risks, to help her die, if that remained her choice. And, if the worst came to the worst, surely she would get hold of one of the available guides and find a gentler way of escaping from the circumstances she found so intolerable. But Martha's last letter said: 'I sat on the window-sill for two hours and I couldn't do it.' Next day, a newspaper recorded her death, by throwing herself from that window. It doesn't need a high level of imagination or sympathy to be horrified. But once she had nerved herself to do it, Martha's ordeal was over and she had managed to go on controlling her own life up to the end.

Many attempts at suicide, made for reasons that most people would think good ones, actually fail, and the sufferer is then often in an even worse plight. Elizabeth was one of these. She was a retired doctor and the widow of another doctor, who had died seven years earlier. Since her husband's death she had said repeatedly that she had no wish to go on into her eighties. She was living in comfortable circumstances, having her own flat as part of her daughter's house, and both her daughter and son-in-law were very fond of her. They all enjoyed each other's company, and the arrangement suited them well, but Elizabeth had arthritis, which was painful and severely limited her mobility, and she had tinnitus, an ear condition that involves the sufferer in 'hearing' constant noise. She had also enjoyed being a doctor and missed her role as a busy and useful professional person. Her hobbies did not compensate her for this.

On her eightieth birthday she injected herself with morphine. She lay unconscious for two days, with her son-in-law and daughter taking turns to watch anxiously by her bedside. On the third day she moaned and appeared to them to be suffering distress, so they sent for her family doctor. He immediately contacted the emergency services. She was rushed into intensive care and after several weeks returned home. Now, she could no longer look after herself and was mentally confused most of the time, but one day, as he fed her, she reduced her son-in-law to tears when she had a brief return to reality and said: 'I made a dreadful mess of it, didn't I?'

When Elizabeth died, at home, some three months later, friends thought that both her carers looked ten years older.

Karen was well into her eighties when she decided that her life was no longer of any value to her. She had been one of a large family, and although she had never married, she had plenty of nephews and nieces who took an interest in her and whose children took the place of grandchildren. She had been a librarian, work that she had enjoyed, and she was well-known for her prize-winning entries into local flower shows, dahlias being a speciality. In her generation car-owning was not an essential, and she was happy to cycle everywhere locally or to use public transport. Her house and its beautiful garden were near a village, itself not very far from the pretty

English market town where she was born. Her peaceful life was shattered by a nasty fall, in which her hip was broken. It did not mend well enough for her to go on living independently and she moved into sheltered accommodation.

After a few months [Karen said] I decided that this wasn't the life for me. Some of my possessions were in my one room but I wouldn't be going back to my own home. And without my garden I felt really lost. My leg is so painful that I can only sit comfortably for short periods, and even then I need painkillers. I hate taking them because they make me confused and muddled in thought. My family and friends visit me, of course, but they are all busy with their own lives. And no one here is capable of intelligent conversation.

My problem was that I am a Christian and I had always been taught that suicide was a sin. That took a lot of thinking about but in the end I decided that since I was nearly 90 God would be calling me home soon anyway and surely He would forgive me, provided I didn't involve anyone else. I waited until a bitterly cold January night – the radio said the temperature was going down to -4. I put on my thinnest nightgown and summer dressing-gown and struggled out into the garden when I was sure everyone had settled down for the night. It was about half-past ten. I lay down among the bushes. I remember hearing the church clock strike as far as two in the morning, then I must have lost consciousness.

Alas for Karen! After all that careful thought and planning, after that dreadful experience of the hours in the bitter cold, she was still alive when the staff found her room empty next morning and searched the gardens. She was rushed into intensive care. Unlike Elizabeth, her condition was no worse after her attempted suicide than it had been before. Three years later she said:

I can't begin to describe how dreadful it felt as I came round and realized that I was recovering into this world. The matron of the home was very angry with me for what I had done. And some of my family, who are more devout Christians than I am, told me that God would be angry with me too. I don't agree with them. But I shan't try again. I had hoped to leave my money mostly to my two favourite charities but it must be used up by now, paying for me to go on with this unhappy existence. It doesn't seem right. I do so look forward to the end.

A lot of research has been done into suicide. It is often claimed in these books and articles that many, if not most, suicides are not serious attempts to die but are really 'cries for help', which the rest of us have been ignoring. They cite as evidence two facts – that there are far more failed suicides than successful ones and that the majority of those who fail the first time do not try again. It may very well be true that many irrational suicides are not meant to succeed. One thinks of the teenager who rushes off and swallows a bottle full of aspirin tablets after a bitter lovers' quarrel. The intention of being rescued in time is often suggested by the leaving of a note or by the fact that the apparent suicide attempt is made in a place where discovery is almost certain.

None of this applies to the rational failed suicides, such as those of Elizabeth and Karen. Moreover, the fact that many failed suicides do not repeat the attempt – remember that the records on which the researchers are working do not distinguish between rational and irrational suicides – may have many explanations. He or she may be too exhausted, physically and mentally, by the first attempt to be capable of trying again or may have used up the only supply of a suitable drug, which is what happened in the following case.

Thomas and his wife were both in very poor health, both needing wheelchairs even to get around their flat, but they *were* managing, just, with a great deal of help from visiting nurses and various neighbours. They were hoping to die together but had not given any thought to the likelihood of this happening. If they had, perhaps they would have been led on to the thought of whether they could do anything about this wish. Probably not, because they were not in the habit of thinking and planning ahead. So Thomas was shattered to find one morning that Gladys had died in her sleep. As soon as the funeral was over, he started hoarding his sleeping tablets, and when he thought he had enough he swallowed the lot. But he had reckoned without his helpful neighbours, one of whom noticed that the bedroom curtains were not closed at night or had not been opened next morning – remember that it takes a long time to die of drugs taken by mouth. When he had been brought round Thomas reported: 'They're giving me my sleeping pills one dose at a time now and standing over me while I swallow them.'

Thomas and Gladys had wanted to die together, an ambition that is quite widely shared by couples who have been amicably married for most of their lives. Some take a more active role and successfully end their lives simultaneously. A few years ago, the sleeping-car attendant on an overnight express from Scotland to London found the bodies of an elderly couple in one of the compartments. There was also a note addressed to whoever found them, apologizing for the shock he was bound to suffer. The husband was a retired and eminent scientist, aged 78, and his wife was 76. One of their sons gave evidence at the inquest that his parents had often discussed their intentions within the family, and that they had devised the plan five years earlier. His father had begun to develop arthritis in his hands, which prevented him from doing day-to-day maintenance about the house and also from playing the bagpipes! More important to him was the fact that he was beginning to get forgetful and confused. The couple had died from cyanide poisoning.

At about the same time in Australia, a couple of similar age and eminence ended their lives together, though not by cyanide. In the United States a researcher found records of 97 cases of simultaneous deaths by elderly couples between 1980 and 1987. A typical case is of a 73-year-old couple living in Kansas. Both were suffering from emphysema (an irreversible and progressive lung disease) and various heart ailments, but they did not want to live in an institution. Walter wrote in his suicide note: 'We have completely run out of energy.' Before their deaths they had laid their plans carefully, including writing their own obituaries for the local paper and paying for their own funerals.

Another couple, Eric and Lotte, this time from California, were in their eighties, in fragile health and blind. A friend said: 'They left taped messages for a lot of people, including the coroner, telling him exactly which drug they had used.' Other friends spoke of their comparative cheerfulness in the last few weeks before they died.

In 1991 Charles, aged 87, and his wife Rena, aged 84, were found dead in their Toronto home by their daughter. There was a letter clearly stating that the decision to end their lives after living together for 59 years was their own, and that their children played no part in their deaths. The daughter who went to their home and found them, after failing to get any answer to her phone calls, said: 'They were lying side by side, looking so peaceful. I couldn't imagine one without the other.'

Returning to England, Arthur Koestler, who had written the introduction to the *Guide to Self-deliverance*, ended his life in 1983 by an overdose of barbiturates. He was 77 years old and suffering from Parkinson's disease and cancer. He had written: 'There is only one prospect worse than being chained to an intolerable existence: the nightmare of a botched attempt to end it.' He was spared that. Koestler's suicide note referred only to his own death, but his wife, Cynthia, who was only 55 years old and in good health, ended her life at the same time, writing in her suicide note that she could not face life without him. This made a double suicide in which one death was a rational escape from an intolerable existence, and the other, apparently, an impulsive act motivated by the devastating prospect of bereavement.

Arthur Koestler had made his support for the legalization of voluntary euthanasia very clear when he became a vice-president of the society set up for that purpose. If it had been legal for his doctor to be there, giving him the drugs that would peacefully end his life, Cynthia would have had to wait at least until the formalities were over before she could take her own life. She would also have been involved in the previous discussions between her husband and the two independent doctors who must have agreed that her husband's euthanasia was voluntary and that he was unwilling to accept any further medical treatment. It is surely not unreasonable to suppose that under those circumstances she might have considered her choice to die more carefully and maybe even have decided, sadly, that she could somehow find the strength to go on living in the hope of better things to come. Obviously we shall never know, but the thought haunted some of those reading about their deaths, forced by law to take place in isolation.

4

What about the doctors we would like to help us?

◇

So far we have only looked at the question of a chosen death from the point of view of the one who would like to have help to die. What about the helper? The patient turns naturally for help to the family doctor, the one who is already playing a major part in his life. Whether the patient is incurably ill with cancer, multiple sclerosis, motor neurone disease, AIDS or any of a large number of other ailments, there will have been a long history of medical treatment by the time voluntary euthanasia comes to mind.

In fact, although the thought may come to the mind of the patient, most do not raise the subject with their doctor, even though they frequently express the wish for an early end to their suffering to the nurses, other carers and their family. They assume that the doctor will not listen to them or that it is improper even to try to talk to a doctor about such things. Some would not want to involve their doctor in breaking the law even if they suspected that he or she might be willing to help them, and, in their turn, doctors tend to assume that because patients do not, on the whole, talk about their wish for help to die, this means that they do not harbour such a wish.

An exception to this general rule was a cancer patient whose case was described by her family doctor in a medical journal a few years ago. She had had hospital treatment, but her cancer was incurable and she was, for the time being, well enough to live at home. 'Well, if I've got cancer,' she said, 'I'm not going to get better am I? So I want you to give me enough tablets so I can see myself off when I'm ready.'

'Did they tell you at the hospital you've got cancer?'

'No, course they didn't. They're not allowed to, are they, because of that oaf.' For a moment the doctor wondered which of his colleagues had sunk so far in her estimation as to be described as an 'oaf', but then he realized it was her pronunciation of 'oath' and that she was referring to the Hippocratic Oath. She thought that it forbade doctors to tell unpleasant truths to their patients. The doctor explained that he was allowed to tell her the truth but that he was not allowed to help her to die. She was asking him to provide the drugs for her to commit suicide, but he could not do that. It turned out that she was an unusually persistent patient, and he was an unusually tolerant doctor. In the end he said: 'All right. You need these sleeping tablets, and I'll give you a prescription for a bottle full. They would almost certainly kill you if you took a lot of them. Now let's look at what can be done in the meantime.'

Several months later she died fairly peacefully, and the spare bottle of pills was found untouched in her cupboard. The doctor's conclusion was that as long as she felt she had an escape route she was willing to go on, making the best of things. He was probably right. Those who want the legal right to choose help to die hope not to have to exercise that right. They just do not like the idea of being made to go on living against their will in what, to them, is indignity. In the United States in 1995 a Death with Dignity Bill presented to the New Hampshire legislative assembly defined suffering as 'a state of severe distress, sense of loss of being a person, lack of hope, loss of control and unacceptably impaired quality of life'. If things never get as bad as that, so much the better.

The idea that the Hippocratic Oath is binding on all doctors is widespread among the general public, although the oath itself is very rarely used nowadays. Those medical schools that still retain it as part of their medical students' qualification ceremony use a greatly scaled-down version. The original, in Greek of course, dates from the fifth century BC, when one of the primary duties of a doctor was to provide an easy death (by means of poison) if he could not heal his patient, but the doctors who gathered around Hippocrates did not agree. The level of medical knowledge and the prevailing religious beliefs were very different, as the following translation shows.

I swear by Apollo Physician, by Asclepius, by Health, by Panacea, and by all the gods and goddesses, making them my witnesses, that I will carry out, according to my ability and judgement, this oath and this indenture. To hold my teacher in this art equal to my own parents; to make him partner in my livelihood; when he is in need of money to share mine with him; to consider his family as my own brothers, and to teach them this art, if they want to learn it, without fee or indenture. I will use treatment to help the sick according to my ability and judgement, but never with a view to injury and wrongdoing. I will keep pure and holy both my life and my art. In whatsoever houses I enter, I will enter to help the sick, and I will abstain from all intentional wrongdoing and harm. And whatsoever I shall see or hear in the course of my profession in my intercourse with men, if it be what should not be published abroad, I will never divulge, holding such things to be holy secrets. Now if I carry out this oath, and break it not, may I gain forever reputation among all men for my life and my art; but if I transgress it and forswear myself, may the opposite befall me.

Picking out the bits that seem to be relevant now, doctors do sometimes raise their commitment to the Oath as an objection to performing voluntary euthanasia. 'I will use treatment to help the sick ... but never with a view to injury or wrong-doing' or 'I will ... help the sick, and I will abstain from all intentional wrongdoing and harm' can be interpreted in this way by doctors.

If 'wrongdoing' means breaking the law, then they are quite right. The law in nearly all countries forbids a doctor intentionally to end the life of a patient. In order for them to do so, the law will have to be changed, which, as we have seen, almost four out of five people think would be a good idea. The evidence of what doctors think about changing the law is not as clear cut. There is not as much research evidence and the results are not as similar from country to country as in the case of ordinary citizens, most of whom, of course, are not doctors. However, it can safely be said that the proportion in favour of legalizing the medical practice of voluntary euthanasia is a good deal lower among doctors.

On the other hand, if by 'wrongdoing' they mean denying a patient the means to an earlier and more merciful death, at that patient's considered request, the Oath tells them they must not do that.

A recent example of the confused state of the medical attitude to this problem comes from Australia. Northern Territory passed the first law allowing medical aid in dying in 1995. The Australian Medical Association campaigned against this, but the President of the AMA has spoken publicly of having assisted two patients to die at their request! Despite this, he said euthanasia should not be legalized and went on to say: 'In the end doctors will continue to do what they believe to be right in the best interests of their patients and his or her immediate family.' At about the same time the spokesman for the much smaller Australian medical group, the Doctors' Reform Society, said: 'It's time politicians stopped running away from the concept of death and allowed dying people the right to choose whether to request medical assistance to end their lives.'

It is interesting to think about why doctors and patients as a whole should have such different attitudes to decriminalizing voluntary euthanasia. After all, at almost every death there are two people at the centre, a dying patient and a doctor, and if the patient were asking for help to die might we not expect the doctor to think: 'This person is suffering and I can do nothing further to relieve his extreme distress. He knows he cannot recover and is asking for my help. Surely the law should not forbid me to give him the drugs that would enable him to die, as he wishes.'

Some doctors do think like that – it was, after all, a group of doctors who felt so strongly about it that they set up the British Voluntary Euthanasia Society in the first place – but apparently such doctors are still in a minority. So how do the rest cope with their inability to respond to their patient's last request – that is, for help to die?

There is no doubt that some doctors take the risk and do it anyway, illegal or not. This is not officially recorded, so no figures are available, but in private conversations and, increasingly, in letters to the medical press, doctors refer to these occasions. In his autobiography, published in 1974, a Scottish doctor, George Mair, described involuntary euthanasia as being common practice in an English hospital in which he had worked soon after he qualified. Elderly people with advanced malignancies were given a large injection of a suitable drug and were asleep within minutes and dead within hours. It was so 'normal', he wrote, that he assumed that English law must be different from Scottish law, which he knew forbade euthanasia. Later, when he realized that it was all illegal, he continued to regard it as merciful: 'It saved them weeks or months of pain, worry and possibly even fear.'

Mair also described the death of another cancer patient, a woman in her forties. She was already on massive doses of pain-killers and had only weeks, perhaps months, to live. She asked him one day to do her a favour. She had put her affairs in order, said her goodbyes to family and friends and now wanted to be put in a side room and to die there while listening to her favourite music. 'I did exactly as she wished. Her last words were whispered but clear, "Thank you. Thank you so very, very much." '

The families and friends of patients whose deaths have been mercifully brought forward by a doctor speak very frequently about their experiences. In fact, it is sometimes suggested that changing the law is unnecessary 'because I'm sure doctors do that, don't they?' This is the way it has been put by 'the man in the street', and it is one interpretation of a frequent remark by doctors during debates on the subject – 'Oh, don't let's bring the law into this.' And most impressively of all, used by Lord Dawson of Penn, the royal physician, in the House of Lords debate on the first Voluntary Euthanasia Bill in 1936. 'This Bill is completely unnecessary,' he said, 'because all good doctors do it anyway.' Fifty years later, when the State papers were released, it emerged that he had recently done it for a rather special patient, George V. It is worth noting that this was not voluntary euthanasia. The king was past voicing an opinion, and Lord Dawson gave his advice to the royal family, presumably Queen Mary and the Prince of Wales (later Edward VIII and later still the Duke of Windsor). The reason was not for the personal benefit of the patient, however. It was in order for the royal death to take place at such a time that it would be announced first in the morning paper, *The Times*. The evening papers were thought to be lacking the necessary dignity for the occasion.

According to law, Lord Dawson was guilty of murder, at that time punishable by hanging. However, the prosecuting authorities were not informed of what he had done and Lord Dawson died at the age of 81 in 1945, having been physician to both Edward VIII and George VI in the meantime.

George V died in 1935. Forty years earlier, the President of the Royal Academy and famous Victorian painter, Frederic, later Lord, Leighton, had also received medical help to die. His death has recently been described: 'It was time to bid the world farewell before the ministration of chloroform rendered him senseless.'

When a patient is dying at home rather than in hospital the doctor is in a much safer position if he or she ignores the law. Provided the patient has been seen by a doctor within the preceding fortnight, the only signature required on the death certificate is the doctor's own, and the cause of death may be recorded as the cancer or whatever illness the patient was dying of. The only people who might complain of the doctor's conduct would be the family, and a family physician is likely to know their views beforehand, even if nothing has actually been said out loud.

In England in 1985, however, a family doctor was charged with attempted murder. The complaint was brought by the hospice from whose care the patient had recently discharged himself. The jury brought in what some people regarded as a perverse verdict. The judge outlined the state of the law for them and that outline, together with the evidence they had heard, clearly pointed to a conviction. Nevertheless, the verdict was 'not guilty'.

It was widely assumed that no English jury would convict a doctor who fell foul of the law by giving voluntary euthanasia, but this assumption was rudely overturned in 1992 by the case of Dr Cox. The doctor was found guilty of attempted murder after a nurse reported to the hospital authorities that he had deliberately ended the life of a patient. Mrs Boyes, who had been his patient for 13 years, suffered from rheumatoid arthritis, the illness in which he specialized. She had frequently asked him to ensure that her death was not agonizing and he had promised to do this. When she reached, in the words of one of the witnesses, the stage of 'howling like a dog', he could find no way of relieving her pain other than the injection that stopped her heart.

The risk of ignoring the law has obviously changed immeasurably since Lord Dawson's time. One would think that an increasing awareness of this would mean that doctors would begin to support changing that law, and there is, indeed, some evidence that such support is increasing, especially among younger doctors. For example, in 1994 a study of British doctors, published in the *British Medical Journal* (*BMJ*), showed that 46 per cent would be willing to consider voluntary euthanasia for a suitable patient, if it were legal. The survey was carried out in Cambridge and was based on replies to an anonymous questionnaire from 312 family doctors and consultants. The figure was 40 per cent in a study of Israeli doctors carried out in 1991. In Australia, 60 per cent of doctors are in favour of changing the law to allow voluntary euthanasia.

There is another objection from the doctor's point of view. Any request for medical treatment that will bring about an early and peaceful death has to come from the patient. If the doctor agrees to do it, there has to be clear evidence that the decision about when it is actually to happen is the patient's. In theory, it has always been the case that doctors only give their patients advice, which the patient either accepts or refuses. In practice, it is so rare for patients to question their doctor's advice that the medical profession, perhaps unconsciously, perceives itself in the role of decision-maker.

This perception is nowhere illustrated more vividly than in the BMA handbook *Euthanasia*. Although it did not pretend to be discussing involuntary euthanasia – it had already defined that as 'culpable homicide' – it quoted the following as an argument against legalizing voluntary euthanasia: 'We shall start by putting patients away because they are in intolerable pain and haven't long to live anyway; and we shall end up putting them away because it's Friday night and we want to get away for the weekend.'

The doctor who said this had clearly not thought of the patient as the decision-maker. It is odd that the eminent philosopher, from whose work the BMA took this quotation, had not noticed his mistake, but it is even more surprising that the BMA committee that wrote the handbook also accepted it as a reasonable consequence of making voluntary – that is, patient-decided – euthanasia legal. The language used – 'putting patients away' – is worth noting, but it is only part of what makes the statement so abhorrent. The slur on the medical profession is every bit as offensive. As one commentator remarked; 'At that rate none of us should ever agree to have surgery on Friday, in case the impatient surgeon removes the wrong bit.'

Dr Robert Twycross is an eminent hospice doctor, the head of one of Britain's earliest and most renowned hospices, Michael Sobell House in Oxford. In *The Lancet* in 1990 he wrote that he would be unable to resist the temptation to move to involuntary assisted death if he were legally allowed to practise voluntary euthanasia.

Involuntary assisted death would remain a crime, of course. Did Dr Twycross mean that he would suddenly become willing knowingly to break the law? The idea is ludicrous to anyone who knows him. Did he mean he would record the involuntary deaths falsely? The idea is unthinkable, for the same reason. It is impossible to know what he meant, but such muddled thinking is fairly typical of the doctors who do not want to be involved with voluntary euthanasia.

The idea that the patient should be the arbiter of his medical fate is making rapid progress, at any rate on paper, in many countries today. This is partly because of an increasing expectation by nearly all of us that, as competent adults, we should be allowed to make our own decisions. The complexity of modern medicine is also leading to a need to share decisions, with nurses, for example, in a way that was once unknown. The patient in the following episode narrowly avoided a premature death by involuntary euthanasia.

'I think care only would be appropriate for this patient, don't you, Sister?' The patient of whom the doctor was

speaking was very old, bed-bound, apparently unconscious and suffering from pneumonia.

'She hasn't expressed any wish to die. I think she
should have antibiotics,' the nurse responded.

'Oh, yes, certainly.'

The patient recovered from her pneumonia, and next
time she saw the Sister she said: 'Thank you for what you
said, Sister. I *am* still enjoying reading my novels.'

The nurse who told this story – and it is only fair to say that
she was a very senior and experienced nurse and that the
doctor in question was not a senior and experienced doctor –
used it to illustrate the fact that apparently unconscious
patients may be able to hear. But it also demonstrates that
doctors are willing to make decisions about non-treatment
without asking if that would be what the patient would prefer.
And the law allows this, even though the patient is likely to
die without the denied treatment. Decisions to stop or not to
offer treatment that would prolong the patient's life are pro-
death decisions, and in the view of those who want patients to
be allowed the choice of medical help to die, these non-
treatment decisions should always be made in consultation
with the patient.

Traditionally the doctor (male) was the decision-maker, and
the nurse (female) carried out his orders. Nowadays doctors
and nurses are viewed as part of a medical team, and this
means that the views of the nurses, individually and expressed in nursing journals and through professional bodies,
are important. A study of nurses' attitudes to euthanasia was
published in 1992 in Australia. This showed that about half
had been asked by incurably ill patients to hasten their deaths
– the same proportion as doctors – and 5 per cent of those
nurses had responded to the patients' requests without being
asked by a doctor to do so. Nearly all had cooperated with
doctors (a quarter of those asked by a patient to hasten death)
who took active steps to help.

About 75 per cent of nurses in Australia would welcome the introduction of guidelines similar to those used in the Netherlands. These guidelines do not refer to the nurse's role in the practice of voluntary euthanasia. The patient is the only one allowed to make the original request, and the giving of the drugs that bring about the death must be done by a doctor. Nevertheless, Dutch doctors speak of listening attentively to nurses during the discussions that lead to the decision to respond to a patient's request, and because they tend to spend more time with and speak more informally with patients, there is a good chance that the patients express their feelings more openly to the nurses.

All those concerned in providing health care, whether doctors, nurses or health-service managers, are routinely confronted with difficult decisions about treatment because of its ever-rising cost. Should the patient's views about this be taken into account? This is an important topic that we shall return to later, but it seems certain that, whether they like it or not, doctors are going to have to accept a lot of shared decision-making, even though many of them look back nostalgically to a time when they were in sole command.

'One of my patients tells me that he intends to take his own life and has asked me the best way to do it. I've just realized that I don't know. All my training was about preserving life.'

The family doctor who spoke these words is clearly one whose patients can talk to him openly without fear of being rebuffed in any way. The patient either did not know that it was a criminal offence to 'aid, abet, counsel or procure a suicide' or he confidently expected his doctor to incur the risk of criminal prosecution on his behalf.

The last comment – 'all my training was about preserving life' – gives us the clue to another important element in the lack of medical support for voluntary euthanasia. The assumption underlying medical education is that it is always better to be alive than dead, no matter what the circumstances, and, of course, 99 per cent of the time this is true. We marvel at the endurance of people such as Terry Waite, who survive being held as a hostage for years, suffering physically and mentally to an extent that we prefer not to try to imagine. We accept as reasonable his belief that even that was better than being dead because he hoped he would eventually be released and return to normality. This hope, however, is not available to patients who know that their disease is incurable and who find their quality of life unendurable.

What a doctor should do when a patient is in this position is something that used not to be considered much when medical students were being taught, and the common practice was to hand over to the nurses at that point. The basic idea was that the doctor's job was to 'cure' and the nurse's job was to 'care'. All this has dramatically changed now that palliative care has become recognized as a distinct branch of medicine, a change that stems largely from the pioneering work of Dame Cicely Saunders, the founder of the British hospice movement. Unfortunately, she and many – perhaps most – of the palliative care doctors refuse to accept that their excellent care is not enough for many patients, grateful as they are to get it. Acute physical pain can usually be abated, and if the worst comes to the worst the patient is kept so sedated as to be unaware of it. Constant nausea and vomiting, breathlessness and a host of other 'discomforts' are harder for both doctor and patient to cope with. But there is, in addition, the mental pain of the indignity of it all, and of having one's dearest wish, for it all to be over, set aside.

One reason for the objections to voluntary euthanasia expressed by palliative care doctors is: 'I don't want to do it.' If only they would say so, and put it so simply, it would be possible, as patients or future patients, to say how much we sympathize. Only warped people want deliberately to bring about the death of another human being. It is hard to accept that having a lethal injection, at his or her own request, is the only remaining good thing that can happen to this patient. It is even harder to realize that, as the patient's doctor, you are the only one with a right to do it, and hardest of all to do it. Those doctors who speak of the experience find it draining.

The doctor's position was made movingly clear in the Dutch film *Death on Request*, which was shown on television in Britain in 1995. Cees van Wendel de Joode was suffering from motor neurone disease, an incurable condition leading to progressive loss of control of the muscles. The average time from diagnosis to death is three years. The well-known British journalist, Jill Tweedie, died in a few months; the world-famous physicist, Stephen Hawkings, has had the disease for many years. Cees said from the beginning that he wanted to die at home, when *he* felt his time had come. Cees and his wife also said that they were willing for a film to be made about his last few months, including his actual death. They knew that the Dutch system of allowing the patient to choose to die like this, with the help of his doctor, is misrepresented by opponents, in the Netherlands itself, and much more so overseas.

It is a moving and dignified film. 'If only we had that choice and control over our own dying,' was one very common reaction. Another was: 'I'd never thought before of the tremendous strain it all is for the doctor.' And indeed Dr van Oyen, the family physician, told us and showed us what an awesome thing it is to do. He was not, however, driven by compassion to do it illegally, and he had to get another independent doctor to check the diagnosis and make sure that Cees understood what he was doing. By carefully observing the code of practice he also knew that, although the prosecuting authorities would check his report of the death, he would not be prosecuted for bringing it about. All this makes it less hard on the doctor.

Fortunately, most deaths are sufficiently short and the preliminary suffering bearable, so a Dutch family doctor performs voluntary euthanasia only about twice in three years. Nevertheless it has never been suggested that doctors must practise voluntary euthanasia, only that they should be allowed to do it. There will be many occasions when the patient who makes the request is not in a condition that seems to the doctor to justify bringing his life to an end. Consider this Dutch woman and her doctor's response.

Clara had been my patient for many years. She came to me one day and said she was utterly tired of living and would I help her to die? She was 83 years old and had a few ailments for which she needed to take various mild drugs. Her sight and hearing were not as good as they had been. But she was living in her own comfortable home, with enough money, well able to take care of herself and with a loving family with whom she was in frequent contact. Her main complaint seemed to be that she was no longer getting much pleasure from her visits to art exhibitions! 'I said 'Certainly not!' and 'Count your blessings', although not in so many words.

Some weeks later she rang me and said: 'I've managed to get some drugs that I'm sure will end my life and I'm about to take them. But I didn't want to do that without saying goodbye. This is the only time as my doctor that you have refused to help me, and I do understand why.'

I said, 'Leave the door unlocked. I'm coming.' When I got there she was drifting into unconsciousness, and I sat with her until she died, then I rang the police. At first they were very angry and wanted to take me into custody. I said, 'What are you going to charge me with? I didn't even prescribe the drugs, let alone administer them.' So in the end they went away.

In some countries the police would have had to charge the doctor with failing to reverse the effect of the lethal drugs his patient had taken. In others, the doctor's duty under these circumstances is undefined, and the police might have charged him with aiding and abetting a suicide. Whether he was prosecuted would depend on the policy of the prosecuting authority.

An American lawyer, working for a prosecuting authority, said at an international conference on medical ethics: 'I've got a city full of crimes out there. Young men with guns are killing each other and innocent bystanders. You think I want to know about good doctors helping sick old people to die?'

We know, however, that the British Crown Prosecution Service took a different view in the case of Dr Cox.

Even if the patient, unlike Clara, is in such a state that the treating doctor thinks, 'If I had reached that stage my dearest wish would be to die, painlessly and fairly soon,' he or she may still have conscientious objections, usually based on religious belief. It has been suggested that in those circumstances doctors should at least tell the patient why they are unwilling to help. They should also make it clear to their patients that they may be able to find a doctor who will help and possibly give the telephone number of an organization able to offer assistance in that search. It must be remembered that patients are likely to be comparatively incapable of much independent action by the time they are getting to the stage of asking for help to die.

The lady who thought that the Hippocratic Oath forbade doctors to tell patients the truth about their medical conditions, especially when the outlook is bleak, is slightly out of date in the case of North America and most of western Europe. Telling the truth, even in these difficult circumstances, is now regarded as the proper thing to do. It is not long, though, since the custom was to tell the family, but not the patient, the diagnosis of an incurable illness, usually cancer. In some cultures, notably in Japan, the question of whether it is right to tell the patient the truth is still a matter of much debate within the medical profession. This custom has the effect of isolating the patient, as the family speaks in hushed tones and out (one hopes) of the patient's hearing of the coming death. There is no opportunity to tell the patient some of the things that ought to have been said long ago but are going to sound very odd now, unless we all openly admit that the patient is not going to live much longer. For example, if a son says: 'I've always been sorry I said such awful things, Mum, when I left home' his mother may well say: 'What on earth are you raking all that up for?' Why, indeed, if no one is talking about the fact that her life is nearly over?

A patient's timid attempts to talk about his or her suspicions of the true state of affairs are also stifled. Another vignette, in front of the television set, 'I suppose this is the last championship match I'll be watching,' may be met by: 'Don't talk like that, Dad. Cheer up. Have a cup of tea/coffee/glass of beer/gin-and-tonic.'

There seem to have been three main ideas behind this custom of keeping incurably ill patients in the dark about their condition. One is that knowing and accepting that they are going to die fairly soon leads them to die earlier than they otherwise would have done. There is some research evidence that a positive attitude to a potentially life-threatening disease leads to a better outcome than refusing treatment and waiting passively for the end. But that stage has passed for the patients we are at present considering. Although it will be better for all concerned if they can accept their imminent death in as tranquil a way as possible, their attitude will not materially affect the progress of their disease.

Another idea, frequently expressed by a leading hospice director, is: 'We must never deprive our patients of hope.' But when asked, 'Hope of what?' there is no reply. Surely the director does not mean a miraculous recovery? Patients so far out of touch with reality as that would not be deterred by a doctor's opinion that their condition was irreversible. Rational and informed patients are mainly hoping to die without undue distress, preferably while they are still capable of knowing their families. This requires that they are given full information by their doctors, not that they are kept in the dark.

A third, often unexpressed, reason why doctors shrink from telling incurable patients the unpalatable truth may be that they do not want to face the strong feelings that such news is almost bound to arouse. This is one of the many aspects of being a good doctor, when a simple hard-and-fast rule will not do. Some patients make it clear, without actually putting it into words, that they prefer not to know. If the doctor persists in telling them, such patients are likely to 'deny' the knowledge, claim afterwards that they were not told, may indeed succeed in suppressing the memory of the conversation – who is to know which? And does it matter? Well, yes. Telling someone they are going to die in the not too distant future needs to be sensitively done, and if it becomes clear that a particular patient really does not want to know such a prognosis, the attempt is best abandoned.

The fact remains, however, that the majority prefer to have the opportunity of facing the truth, however unpalatable. Being screened from it offends their sense of personal dignity, as though they are not fully adult. How can doctors be prepared for this burdensome role as the bringer of bad news? We are back to the difficulty of fitting new elements into medical education – in this case, effective communication skills. Fortunately, topics like these, as well as broader questions of medical ethics, are increasingly being taught. Clearly it will be no use teaching doctors how to say 'You've got cancer' acceptably, instead of teaching them how to diagnose the cancer in the first place. They have to be able to do both. The problem is somewhat eased now that the concept of continuing education is so general. Learning is no longer seen as something you do before you start work, but as something that you go on doing throughout your working life. In-service training courses are increasingly common now for family doctors and a good place to discuss ethical issues as they arise in relation to real patients.

In the United States the idea of doctor-assisted suicide is widely discussed. The idea is that doctors will be allowed to prescribe appropriate drugs, knowing that their patients intend to use them to commit suicide. As long as a patient administers them, the doctor will be able to feel one step away from the death, compared with actually giving the fatal injection. Another consideration, apart from sparing the doctor's feelings, is that patients may more easily change their minds right up to the last moment when no one else is involved in the act.

Doctors sometimes argue that being allowed to practise active euthanasia would change their role from being a doctor to being an executioner. In fact, some have suggested that going around ending lives should become a separate profession, an idea that we are surely not intended to take seriously. Be that as it may, if the medical profession accepts aiding suicide more readily than it accepts giving voluntary euthanasia, then patients will be grateful.

There are, however, obvious disadvantages from the patient's point of view. Few of those who judge their quality of life to be unacceptable, and whose doctors agree with them, will be capable of injecting themselves, and as we have seen, drugs taken by mouth are slow and uncertain in their action by comparison. This difficulty has been overcome in the United States in recent years by Dr Jack Kevorkian, who has devised a means of injection that the patient can control. The needle is inserted professionally and is connected to the drug supply, which is released when the patient presses a switch. This procedure took advantage of the fact that most of the laws governing end-of-life issues are state laws rather than federal laws, and in Michigan aiding a suicide was not formerly a crime. A law making it a crime was recently passed, but this has not stopped Dr Kevorkian. He is usually portrayed in the media as sinister, dubbed 'Dr Death' and shown in photographs that are lit and chosen to make him look threatening. Nevertheless, an article in the *British Medical Journal* in June 1996 described him as a hero, a man of action, who has taken on the legal, medical and religious establishments.

Of course, one would much prefer to die at home, being helped by one's own doctor and with one's family around. But if travelling to another state and dying alone is the price that has to be paid, some determined people will find the energy and courage to do it. Dr Kevorkian's first suicidal patient had developed Alzheimer's disease at an unusually early age – she was 52 years old when she died. Her family sympathized with her wish not to go on losing the use of her brain and helped her to travel from Oregon to Michigan. After being connected to the apparatus, she pushed the button and received an injection, from the effects of which she died painlessly six minutes later. That was in 1990. In the next six years Dr Kevorkian has helped 42 other people who were incurably ill and did not want to go on struggling to keep alive.

Doctors in North America have been the ones most in the habit of using every death-delaying procedure as it has been developed, without giving sufficient consideration of the benefit to the patient. Cardio-pulmonary resuscitation (CPR), for example, came about as a result of research on behalf of one of the big American electricity companies. Some of the fit young men who worked with cables carrying thousands of volts, from time to time accidentally received massive electric shocks, which stopped their hearts. If some way could be found to start those hearts beating again, before the lack of blood, especially to the brain, had caused too much damage, they would be able to carry on with their young lives again, more or less as they were before the accident. The research was successful, and in no time at all CPR was being routinely given, whenever anyone's heart stopped beating and wherever the treatment was available. Remember Fiona's husband who died of his heart condition after being resuscitated five times? That was in New Zealand.

At the annual congress of the Royal College of Nursing in 1990 a nursing lecturer from Northern Ireland said: 'CPR has been practised for 30 years and in that time some of us have learned that we may be merely prolonging dying rather than bringing people back to life.' At the same meeting a senior nurse from a London hospital said she had been asked to resuscitate an unconscious woman who was 98 years old. The doctor was incredulous when she questioned this decision.

Nevertheless, it is in the United States that the technique of CPR, along with tube-feeding and ventilators, has been used most widely. One contributory factor has been the fact that suing doctors – or anyone else, for that matter – is so much more common there than in other countries. In order to be sure that they will not be accused of neglecting a dying patient, doctors have tended to ask the family: 'Do you want us to do everything we can for him?' This is a question that tends to receive the answer 'Yes' almost automatically. Recently, however, there has been a case in which the family lost its claim that the permanently unconscious elderly mother, suffering from many serious conditions, should have been kept alive as long as possible on a ventilator.

The cost of treating increasingly elderly patients with every possible treatment has escalated to the point where even the world's wealthiest country is having to consider whether this is sensible behaviour. No doubt this is one reason that most of the debate about doctor-assisted suicide is taking place in the United States.

5
Where do the family and friends come in?

◇

It used to be accepted that, as they grew older, people would move into the home of a daughter or son and form part of an extended family. The most usual reason for this was economic necessity; it was rarely the choice of those who could continue to pay for and run their own households. This is now a much less common practice. Commentators in the industrially advanced nations frequently cite this as proof that their own countries have become non-caring societies, and they speak of the extended family as though it were an ideal living arrangement. Of course, it can be, with the grandparents respected for their wisdom and able to take pleasure in their grandchildren. It can, however, also be a source of conflict and constraint, depending on the personalities and circumstances of the family. The system has tended to work best in rural communities, where people often have more living space than in the crowded cities. Wealthy people have always been able to cope better, with bigger houses and sometimes servants to help look after grandparents as they became more frail. Having a climate that makes it possible to spend a large part of the day out of doors also lessens the inevitable strains of mixed generations living together.

Nowadays, even in India and South America, the extended family is becoming less common, as young people move to the cities to look for work. And we should not forget that a quarter of the world's population lives in China, which is trying to avoid having an even higher share by its 'one child, one family' policy. Where will the next generation of Chinese find their extended family?

Fortunately, not living in the same household does not mean being out of touch with one's family. Towards the end of their lives the majority of elderly people get most of the care they need from family members, even in the allegedly un-caring societies of North America and western Europe. In the United States amazing numbers of middle-aged men and women frequently fly to distant parts of their large country, helping their old parents or other family members to cope. As long as the ageing parents are capable of looking after them-selves, few problems arise, but slowly more and more help is needed. The one doing most of the caring, usually a spouse or daughter, can find themselves living in virtual slavery – that is, with no choice of occupation, no wages and precious little off-duty time.

> When she was 70 years old Mrs Hepworth moved into her own little flat, which had been cleverly adapted in the house belonging to her daughter and son-in-law. Now that their children had left home the remainder of the house was large enough for the two of them. For many years the arrangement worked beautifully, but by the time Mrs Hepworth died, aged 91, it looked as though her daughter might die first from overwork. Two nurses arrived every morning to get the old lady out of bed, washed, dressed, toileted and settled in front of her television set. Then it was 'over to you, Gillian' for the rest of the 24-hour care. It was heavy work, lifting her on and off the commode every two hours, and back into bed in the evening. David, her son-in-law, had a back injury,

which prevented him helping with lifting. Mrs Hepworth no longer spoke or seemed to show interest in television or recognize family members. Gillian had to provide all her meals, of course, and usually had to get up to answer her bell at least once in the night. For the last year or two of her life Mrs Hepworth was taken into a nursing home for a fortnight every three months, and Gillian's life centred around planning for, and looking forward, to those breaks from her punishing routine.

When one of the nurses said cheerily one morning, 'We've brought her anti-flu injection to-day,' it was all Gillian could do not to say out loud: 'Please don't give it to her. It would be such a relief to us both if she died of flu.' She had been very fond of her mother and felt guilty even thinking such a thing.

George's case was rather different, although he had also reached his nineties. He was living with his son and daughter-in-law and spent a month each summer in a nursing home, while his carers (who were themselves pensioners) had two weeks' holiday and two weeks at home by themselves. He could still go out for a walk every day, and his mind was still clear. However, he fairly frequently said how tired he was of living on, now his wife and most of his friends were dead, and he had started to lose some control of his bladder, which he found humiliating.

One spring, the social services provider said that George would not be able to have his month in the nursing home – 'He isn't ill enough.' George, of course, was no better than he had been the previous year, somewhat worse, in fact, and what the social services department meant was that other, more seriously deprived old people were getting ahead of him in the queue. The son and daughter-in-law were in despair and consulted the family doctor. He said, 'Let's check on George's medication.' Like many older people, George was taking quite a selection of pills to treat various slight malfunctions, and his doctor suggested that he stop taking them all. George died very peacefully about ten days later, with the doctor taking no further part in his care except to check that the withdrawal of his medication did not cause him distress.

In the cases of Mrs Hepworth and George the families were involved in physically unremitting hard work, but things are a great deal worse when dementia is involved. A few years ago an English school was holding a one-day conference for 17- and 18-year-olds on life-and-death issues. It was 'abortion' in the morning and 'voluntary euthanasia' in the afternoon. The speaker in favour of allowing the choice of help to die for incurably ill patients was followed by a local family doctor, who apologized for his late arrival. The speaker in favour of voluntary euthanasia was considerably startled by the doctor's description of what had delayed him, and still more by what he thought ought to be done about it. He said:

> *I've just been visiting a patient. Actually his wife is my patient, but he's the one I'm worried about. They're both in their eighties, and she has Alzheimer's disease. She can no longer do anything for herself except eat. She can no longer speak. She makes grunting noises like a pig, and grabs and shovels her food into mouth like one, too. In fact in my view she has lost her human characteristics. Her soul is dead.*
>
> *Her husband won't hear of her being taken into a home to be cared for. He insists on looking after her himself. He was in good health when all this started, but now I'm afraid he'll die first.*
>
> *We, as a society, have got to tackle the problem of ending the lives of people in the last stages of senility.*

The reason the other speaker was so startled was that this doctor was advocating involuntary euthanasia. This patient was long past the point of being able to choose for herself, but none of the organizations that are trying to change the law to allow voluntary euthanasia is even willing to talk about making that decision about someone else's life. In their view, most people would make that decision for themselves, if only they knew it was possible to do so.

Perhaps it will eventually be possible to draw up guidelines that will enable the family and doctors together to make such a decision. This would correspond to what happens in the case of grossly handicapped newborns, and it would have to be very tightly controlled. In the meantime, encouraging everyone who hates the idea of suffering from Alzheimer's disease to complete an advance directive seems a better way forward, and some Alzheimer patients in the Netherlands have had their lives mercifully ended on that basis.

It is sometimes suggested that no one need dread becoming senile simply because the afflicted person no longer realizes what is happening to them and sometimes appears quite contented. The thought of changing into that unaware person is not acceptable to many of us, and quite often, in any case, the sufferer varies in the degree of awareness and seems always unhappy. Felicity's disease took this course.

Felicity had always been as tall as her husband and rather more heavily built. She developed Alzheimer's disease and gradually lost her memory and reasoning ability, while remaining in good physical health. In previous ages this condition was known as second childhood, and some of her behaviour was like that of a two-year-old having a temper tantrum. For example, she would stand violently swinging the sitting-room door backwards and forwards if the other people present were paying her no attention. At that stage she could still speak, although conversation was difficult because her memory had largely gone. Later, she had to have sedative drugs to calm her agitation and eventually had to be admitted to a nursing home. By this time she hardly spoke, but occasionally she would manage a few meaningful words. They were 'I want to die,' but she died more than a year after the last time she spoke those words.

After her death it took a major effort for Felicity's friends to remember her as the excellent mother and hostess she had been, and only the oldest of her grandchildren could remember as a loving grandmother. One of the saddest things about a long-delayed death is the way this image of the degraded person overrides the memories of them as they really were for most of their lives.

Sometimes the condition of the loved family member becomes so dreadful that the parents, spouses or grown-up children can bear it no longer. If they then end the suffering life, the act is usually described as a 'mercy killing'.

Andrew, who was 25, and Nicola, who was 21, were visiting their mother daily in the hospital where she was dying slowly of her breast cancer, which had spread to her bones. The breast itself was covered with dressings, but nothing overcame the smell from the breast, which was becoming gangrenous. Pauline was in agony while these dressings were changed and when her toileting needs were attended to, despite the steady supply of pain-killer that was pumped into her arm. She spoke to her children of her wish that it was all over, and at the end of one visit they turned the pump control up as far as it would go. They made no attempt to conceal from the nursing staff what they had done. They were immediately arrested and held in separate police cells for three days, hoping that every approaching footstep was someone coming to tell them their mother was dead. She lived for twelve more days, having been given a drug that would counter the effects of the merciful overdose her children had given her.

The duty solicitor proved to be very active on their behalf, getting them out on bail and persuading the magistrates to reverse their first ruling, that they were not to be allowed to visit their dying mother. They stood trial for attempted murder many months later. Their counsel advised them that they would get more lenient sentences if they pleased 'guilty', and Andrew in particular found this hard to do. 'Murder would be if I got into a fight outside a pub and pulled a knife on somebody. Our mother had done all she could to help us all our lives, and we were trying to do the only thing for her that she really wanted.' Their sentence was twelve months' conditional discharge.

Following the trial, Andrew and Nicola took part in a television programme, which was followed by a phone-in. The lines were jammed. The system for this type of phone-in is one phone number for 'yes' and another for 'no'. The question put to the television audience was: 'Do you think the law should be changed so that doctors can help dying patients to die, if that is their wish?' Of the thousands who rang in, 93 per cent said 'yes'. The opponents of our having control over our own dying say: 'Well, of course, they would, after seeing such an emotive programme.' They imply that we should not be moved by the plight of those who suffer under the present law. In fact, practically all social reform has come about by the efforts of people who were sufficiently upset by individual examples of human suffering to act to improve matters. And if this involved changing the law, then eventually they got it changed.

A long deterioration towards death most often happens to old people, but families frequently have to face dreadful predicaments because of their sons or daughters.

When Emily was born she was so handicapped that the doctors told her parents that she would live for only a few years. She was 32 years old when she died or, rather, when her father killed her. She was never able to speak or walk, to feed herself or to become toilet-trained. She lived at home and, although they had some outside help, her parents' life for 32 years consisted of looking after Emily. Then her father developed a life-threatening heart condition, and her mother was not going to be able to look after her husband and daughter. Emily showed no positive signs of affection towards her parents, but she did always cringe away from strangers and hated any change from her routine. The thought of her misery if they had to put her into a nursing home was more than her parents could face.

'I put sleeping pills into her evening advocaat. That was her favourite drink. When she was asleep I put a pillow over her face until she stopped breathing.'

'Why do you say "I"? Didn't your wife know about it?'

'Oh, yes. She did. We talked about it for a long time beforehand. No, we agreed that if it counted as murder it would be better for only one of us to go to prison.'

This sort of event is usually called a 'mercy killing', but legally it counts as murder. Defending counsel enters a plea of 'not guilty' because of diminished responsibility, and the usual sentence, as in this case, is three years' probation. Sometimes it is a two-year suspended sentence or a conditional discharge.

Diminished responsibility means not being sufficiently in control of yourself to be responsible for your actions. It is certainly not a good description of the state of mind of Emily's parents, although sometimes this could well describe the impulsive action of someone acting alone and in response to the stress of caring for the suffering relative. This was the situation in which Tony found himself.

At 5pm on 2 January 1988 Tony walked into a Manchester police station in a distressed state. Shaking and speaking with great difficulty, he said: 'I killed my wife this morning.' As he was being driven to his flat, he said repeatedly, 'It was the last straw.'

Tony and Esther had been briefly married nearly twenty years earlier, having met in Manchester while Esther was on holiday there. Esther soon returned to her home in Glasgow and they were divorced. There was a son, David, whom Tony never met. Each re-married, but both these marriages also ended in divorce, although Tony remained in contact with Sarah, his daughter by his second marriage. Esther was one of four sisters, the oldest of whom died of Friedrich's ataxia after many years of gradual deterioration from this wasting disease. By the time Tony and Esther met and married again, she, too, had developed the disease and was already in a wheelchair. They had never resolved the problem of which city they would live in, but Esther agreed to move to Manchester for what proved to be the rest of her life. Through a housing association, they got a flat that was specially adapted for the use of someone in a wheelchair.

Tony devoted all his time to looking after Esther, who now had heart trouble and whose speech was very badly impaired, in addition, of course, to remaining completely physically dependent on him. She had been confined to a wheelchair for 12 years, and she had seen her older sister die of the disease from which she was suffering. Her only son was now living in Manchester – the main reason she had agreed to the move – but he refused to have any contact with her, and she was envious of Tony's affectionate relationship with his daughter from the intervening marriage. Even before the move south she had several times said to her doctor that her 'life wasn't worth living'. On numerous occasions she said to Tony, 'Don't let me be like Joan. End it for me.' Tony suggested that she talk to the doctor about it, but Esther refused because she was frightened of going into hospital and being kept there.

Esther was irritable and not sleeping well. Over Christmas she behaved normally in company, but reverted continually to asking Tony to end her life whenever they were alone.

This background information is taken from the transcript of Tony's trial. Now we go on with the account of the then Chairman of the Voluntary Euthanasia Society.

In the autumn of 1988 a member of VES sent us a newspaper account of Tony's trial, at which he was convicted of murder. A life sentence had followed automatically. The trial judge recommends to the Home Secretary how many years that should be – his tariff – but at that time no one else was informed, unless the judge made his recommendation in court. He did not do so in this case. The minimum tariff would be seven years.

The VES member was incensed that a man should receive a life sentence for a mercy killing and offered to pay the costs of his appeal. This put the VES committee in a quandary. It could not ignore its member's request, but it did not want to give the impression that it stood for the legalization of mercy killings [of which, for various reasons, the VES is not in favour]. Its solution was to allow me, the Chairman, to act in my personal capacity, keeping the Committee informed of progress and, via the Newsletter, letting the members know too.

It turned out that Tony qualified for Legal Aid, so a fund for that was not necessary, but the members did subscribe to a fund that would help him a little to make a fresh start when he was released. They also wrote to him in prison, something that he found wonderfully sustaining.

Tony and his parents, Dot and Fred, were anxious to have nothing to do with VES until after his appeal in May 1989, which I attended. I protested to his solicitor about the fact that Tony had been held in prison on remand between January, when Esther died, and his trial in July. It is more usual for alleged mercy-killers to be allowed bail. But when I met his parents later and put this point to them, Dot said: 'Oh it was the best place for him. If you could have seen the state he was in. He wasn't safe [from committing suicide, was the unspoken end of the sentence].'

The usual plea by mercy killers is guilty of manslaughter, by reason of diminished responsibility. At his trial, Tony had pleaded guilty to manslaughter, by reason of provocation. At that time provocation was defined as a sudden loss of self-control, leading to a murderous and violent attack on the victim. Since that time the definition has been extended to cover cases where the accused has been provoked by a long period of misery caused by the person they kill. They have been women who have suffered from domestic brutality. Possibly Tony's circumstances would have been regarded nowadays as constituting provocation. At the time of his trial he would have had to have attacked and killed Esther violently in a furious rage to plead provocation successfully. Smothering her with a pillow because he couldn't bear to look at her, with his hands round her throat, even though she put her hands over his and said 'Don't stop', and all this done in a spirit of worn-out, exhausted giving-in at last to her repeated demand for his help to die. This was not provocation.

The judge explained all this to Tony's counsel and said that the manslaughter defence had failed and his client's only alternative now was to plead guilty to murder. Tony did not realize that he need not accept the advice of his counsel, nor that he would forfeit his right to trial by jury if he pleaded guilty. He did as he was told.

The jury was dismayed to be dismissed from the case at the opening of the second day and signed a letter of protest to the judge. This is a very rare event, in itself. It did no good, of course. By that time the judge had pronounced the life sentence. Tony was transferred to a maximum-security prison pending his appeal. This came ten months later.

Lord Chief Justice Lane, dismissing the appeal, referred to 'this tragic case' but made no attempt to interpret the law mercifully. I wept in court, not just for Tony, but for the sorry state of the law, with all its trappings, that could not find a way to correct any of the many mistakes that had been made in the handling of this case. But at least the embargo on my making any efforts on his behalf was now lifted.

I visited Tony in prison and thus met his parents and older daughter. I wrote to the MP for the area where Tony had lived and also to the MP for the city in which he was imprisoned, asking them to write to the Home Secretary. Both those MPs were in the Opposition party. After a month I wrote again asking if they minded if I wrote to my own MP, a member of the party in power. They were not as shocked as I was by the lack of response from the Home Office, having met it before, but said by all means try your MP. By sheer fluke this man happened to be at that time a junior minister in the Home Office. Within a few days of my letter Tony was told that the procedure was beginning that would lead to his release. That procedure takes three years, one year in a less secure prison, one in an open prison and one in approved lodgings. In the normal course of events it would not have been started for another four years. So in the end he got out four years earlier than he would have done.

As well as writing letters, I had been talking about his case to illustrate the fact that legalizing voluntary euthanasia might reasonably be expected to cut down on mercy killings. One of the journalists' articles written after such an interview was published in a women's magazine and focused almost entirely on Tony's case. This aroused such pity and indignation in one reader that she started visiting Tony in prison and they were married while he was still a prisoner. So far this has proved to be a very happy marriage.

Tony spent four years in prison as a consequence of finally responding to his suffering wife's repeated pleas for help to die. Her death was quick and gentle.

Less than a year before, also in Manchester, a 24-year-old son had stabbed his mother, who was dying of cancer. She survived the stabbing and died of her cancer a month later. The son was found guilty of attempted murder and given two years' probation. The trial report makes no mention of the mother's wishes.

> At the time that Tony's appeal was being dismissed in London, a judge in Cardiff was trying Phillipa for the attempted murder of her mother. Mrs Monaghan had spoken to all her four daughters of her wish to die now that her motor neurone disease had reached the stage at which she could no longer use her arms. Phillipa finally gave her mother pills (which the subsequent post-mortem showed did not cause death) and then put a plastic bag over her mother's head and a pillow over that. After the death, Phillipa was briefly admitted to a psychiatric hospital to prevent her from committing suicide. The judge put her on probation, saying: 'I think you have suffered enough. You are obviously a caring and loving person. You did what you did because you didn't want your mother to suffer.'

It is hard to imagine two more similar cases than Tony's and Phillipa's, or two more contrasting treatments of the offenders. In both cases, the primary wrong is that relatives should be constrained by law to undergo such awful experiences. But Tony's case also shows how hollow is the claim that there is no need for law reform because mercy killers are treated leniently under the present system.

> On average, about two cases a year come before the British courts. Because they are almost always reported to the police by the family member or members who did it, there is no means of knowing how often it happens. By definition the one who dies is, in one way or another, in

poor health and his or her death does not come as a surprise to the family doctor. This was certainly the case for Mrs Jones. She was so ill that her death would certainly have been reported as a natural death if her son had not reported what had actually happened.

Mr Jones was nursed at home and died of cancer. During the months of caring for him and seeing his slow decline, Mrs Jones had been staunchly supported by her son and two daughters. 'You wouldn't let me go on to the bitter end like poor Dad, would you? Promise me you'd help me,' was something she said to any one of them from time to time, but more often to her son.

'Don't talk like that, Mum. When all this is over we'll take you away for a lovely holiday. Let's talk about that.' But by the time Dad died, Mrs Jones was far from well and, to their horror, the adult children heard that she too had developed a cancer. Instead of taking her away for her promised holiday they continued with their spell of nursing. As her condition deteriorated, her son remembered what she had asked him and checked whether she still felt the same. She did, and soon afterwards indicated that she had had enough. He, too, ended her life by smothering her.

He was allowed bail but had to report to the police station every evening. He was an upright, law-abiding man and found this humiliating. He was employed by a public authority, which sent him a very unsympathetic letter referring to his 'serious crime'. It seemed at first that they would dismiss him, even before he had been tried. He appealed to his MP, a man who does not support voluntary euthanasia but is a very devout Christian, who acted at once on Mr Jones's behalf. He got the unpleasant letter withdrawn; no doubt the reminder that the accused is innocent until proved guilty was enough. But both the daily reporting and the threatening letter added to the sufferings of the family, already doubly bereaved. When the trial eventually took place, the sentence was two years' probation.

In some of these cases of stricken families, the suffering person is still capable of ending his or her own life. All he or she needs from close relatives is an acceptance of the decision and a willingness to allow it to happen. Having gone through all the emotional distress of accepting the death of a beloved wife or husband, son or daughter, the survivor is likely to be charged with aiding and abetting a suicide. The maximum sentence is 14 years' imprisonment. This offence was created in Britain in 1961, when suicide was itself decriminalized, and there have been few prosecutions. In both cases when a custodial sentence was imposed, it was of two years. This has not stopped judges haranguing parents about the wickedness of what they have done, and saying that they really should go to prison but will instead receive a lesser sentence.

Many young men go through a period of passionate devotion to their motor cycles, and most of their parents are aware of the road accident statistics. Riders of motor cycles figure as a disproportionately large group among the quadriplegics – that is, people whose spine has been broken at the neck. The quadriplegic's mind is unaffected, but he (less often she) has no control over any part of his body, but his head. It is the nightmare fear that even the most down-to-earth mother has difficulty squashing if she wakes in the small hours and realizes that her son is not yet home.

In Britain in 1985 the parents of Robert were found not guilty of murder but guilty of manslaughter by reason of diminished responsibility. After his accident Robert had begged them to end his life. Twice they gave him what all three hoped would be a lethal dose of drugs, but he survived. Finally they suffocated him. They were put on probation for two years.

'It was a matter of not letting our son down. If we had

faced prison for the rest of our lives it would not have stopped us. Our love for our son overcame this.' These were the father's words as he left the court with his wife. Few would think they demonstrated diminished responsibility, which is the legal fiction that enabled them to walk free.

In another case, only the father was charged. His daughter was herself a qualified and senior nurse. She was battling against cancer, then discovered she was also developing multiple sclerosis. When things got to the point when she decided not to go on, it was the car exhaust that she decided to use. By this time she needed help to do it and her father gave it. In court he said: 'I loved my daughter very much, and if she had wanted to live I would have helped her to live. But she wanted to die, so I helped her to die. I was quite prepared to go to prison for it.'

The minority, who have never been part of a family or who have lost touch with them, usually find friends of some sort who will step in when there is a crisis, even if the 'friendship' has only arisen through a volunteer scheme. Molly, who helped Pearl to commit suicide, had met her through a befriending organization.

In December 1994 a 71-year-old childless widow was visited in hospital by a young woman who had been her home help for the past five months. The patient died soon afterwards, and her friend was charged with attempted murder. Mrs C had lung and throat cancer, the pain from which was being controlled by a drip of diamorphine. She had lost the sight of one eye ten years before and had little remaining sight in the other. A few years before she had had a fall and broken her hip.
  Fifteen months later, minutes before her trial began,

the friend was told that the prosecuting authorities had decided it was not 'in the public interest for the trial to proceed'. The judge spoke approvingly of the extent to which the prosecution service had gone in the case. The results of the post-mortem were inconclusive and further tests were undertaken. The trial had been expected to last five days. After all that, and after having it hanging over her for more than a year, this friend would have received a nominal sentence, the judge said.

For most people it will be a husband, wife or daughter who bears the brunt of the care and who copes with the approaching death, the death itself and its aftermath. These will be the people we have in mind as 'family', but friends, whether peripheral or replacing relatives, as in the case of homosexual couples, should not be forgotten.

The feeling among close relatives that doctors should do something to end their patients intolerable suffering is not new. The great French composer, Hector Berlioz, wrote in 1850 about the death of his older sister from cancer.

My beloved Adèle, my other sister, nearly died herself from exhaustion and the horror of watching this long martyrdom. Yet no doctor dared have the humanity to end it once and for all with a little chloroform. They use it to spare patients the pain of an operation which lasts a few seconds, but they will not consider using it to save them six months of torture, when it is absolutely certain that no remedy, not even time, will cure the disease, and death is clearly the only remaining boon, the sole source of happiness.

Most deaths do not cause the sufferers or their relatives and friends the sort of anguish described in these cases. But many come at the end of such a long drawn-out deterioration that the survivors have difficulty remembering the dying person as he or she was in good health. Deaths described as 'a blessing' or 'a happy release' mean that for some time beforehand it has been realized that death was the only remaining good thing that could happen. If the patient has shared that view, it is small wonder that relatives are sometimes driven by their sympathy to take the law into their own hands.

It is sometimes suggested by opponents that bereaved relatives will be overcome by guilt and remorse after voluntary euthanasia. The evidence from the Netherlands, where they can speak openly about their experiences, suggests the exact opposite. The survivors are, of course, sad – there is no getting over the pain of saying goodbye for the last time – but with a chosen death, there is at least the opportunity to talk a little, knowing it is the last time. And afterwards families say 'She was so calm. It helped us to have a good memory of her' and 'We felt so proud of him. *He* was comforting us, and helping us to accept it.'

In other countries the illegality of the doctor's help means that the relatives' reactions are rarely recorded. The only occasion in which they are on public record is when Mrs Boyes's sons expressed their gratitude to Dr Cox at his trial.

We shall all die, and in the meantime most of us will suffer bereavement. One way and another, we all stand to benefit by gaining more control over the circumstances of our deaths.

6

Religion is against voluntary euthanasia, isn't it?

◇

'I intend to call my next book "Love Thy Neighbour as Thy Dog".' The speaker was referring to the fact that it is a crime to give a merciful death to an incurable and suffering neighbour, but you are allowed to do this for your dog. In fact, you can be prosecuted if you deny this compassionate treatment to your dog.

The words were spoken a few years ago by a young American priest. He belonged to the Episcopal church. In Britain this is closest to the Church of England; elsewhere non-extreme Protestantism would probably best describe its position. The fact that he was advocating mercy killing from the platform of a public conference startled his audience which consisted mainly of doctors and nurses. There is a general assumption that religion is 'against' voluntary euthanasia, but the position is not so simple.

Before we look at what religion has to say about voluntary euthanasia in general, it will be worth thinking about the puzzle that this priest was drawing to our attention. Why should there be such a difference in the way we treat a suffering and incurably ill animal and the way the law requires us to behave to a human being in the same position? If there has to be a difference, should we be more compassionate to the human being or to the animal? These are precisely the sort of questions that religious experts, theologians, have debated throughout the ages.

Jack, who went so unwillingly into hospital to die, said bitterly during his seven weary weeks there, 'They'd be prosecuted if they did this to a dog.' He was quite right. Denying a swift, merciful death to a suffering and incurably ill dog is a punishable offence.

When this problem is put to those who oppose making voluntary euthanasia an option towards the end of life, they commonly reply: 'Ah, but man isn't an animal. He has an immortal soul.' There are many people who would not accept one or the other or both of these statements. But even if we grant that most of us do regard people as significantly different from animals, surely it follows that we ought to treat them better than animals, not worse. How can treating people with more humanity than animals mean denying them the merciful death for which they are asking?

There appears to be no sensible explanation for the present state of affairs. The fact that it goes on, unchallenged, can be due only to a failure to think clearly and afresh. The weight of tradition, inertia and an unwillingness to disturb established practice all combine to oppose new ideas and proposals for radical change. Nowhere is this more evident than in religion.

Most religions base their beliefs on an ancient text. In the West this is usually the Bible; in the Islamic world it is the Koran. These texts obviously have nothing to say about modern medicine, and when the various religious authorities produce statements about the problems and choices that arise from the practice of modern medicine, they are interpreting the texts. Moreover, they are often working from translations of those texts. It is small wonder that there is so much division between those who claim to base their beliefs on the same text. It becomes almost meaningless to say 'Christians believe . . .' when we know that the various factions in Northern Ireland all regard themselves as good Christians who believe in God.

For practical purposes, the most important religions to consider in relation to voluntary euthanasia are Christianity and Judaism. This is because the countries where there are strong movements to legalize its careful practice are in North America, western Europe and the countries of the British Commonwealth.

Suicide is generally agreed not to be forbidden in the Bible. It was declared a mortal sin by the church in the fifth century AD. By the fifteenth and sixteenth centuries, ideas about medicine were among those that Europe gradually rediscovered, as knowledge of the world of ancient Greece and Rome spread throughout Europe. It is interesting that the Christian church did not adopt the Greek and Roman view that rational suicide could be admirable. Pythagoras, Plato and Aristotle all accepted it in the case of incurable illness, and Seneca wrote: 'Why should I endure the agonies of disease when I can emancipate myself from all my torments? If I know that I must suffer without hope of relief I will depart, not through fear of pain itself, but because it prevents all for which I would live.' Instead, the church authorities chose as their model of appropriate behaviour for doctors Hippocrates, a man who opposed the accepted view of most of his contemporaries that it was part of a doctor's duty to offer poison to an incurable and suffering patient.

In the modern world it is rare for the law of the land to be based exclusively on the doctrines of one religious belief, and most democracies incorporate religious tolerance into their constitutions. For more than a thousand years, however, the law throughout Europe was based on the doctrine of the Roman Catholic church. The law forbidding suicide remained on the statute books for a long time, even after the Protestant churches were established in the sixteenth century. In Germany, suicide was decriminalized in 1751, and most other European countries have since followed suit.

Nevertheless, despite the decriminalization, the stigma that attaches to suicide has meant that the inquest that follows a suspicious death makes every effort to avoid bringing in a verdict of suicide. In the Catholic Republic of Ireland, for example, even the most obvious suicides used to be pronounced accidental deaths. This practice has recently changed, and Ireland's published suicide rate is now much the same as the United Kingdom's. In both countries, however, the reluctance to admit that death was self-chosen remains. In Oxford in 1989, for example, a 65-year-old man was found dead in his flat, with a plastic bag over his head. He had been suffering from a serious heart condition and had made a will shortly before his death. The coroner recorded an open verdict. Even when it is clear that it is a death by suicide, it is customary to add 'while the balance of his/her mind was disturbed'. Over a hundred years ago the medical journal *The Lancet* commented: 'For a jury to impute insanity to a man without any evidence beyond the bare fact of suicide is an unworthy evasion.'

In spite of this, Britain's leading forensic scientist, Bernard Knight, in his standard textbook for medical students, which was published as recently as 1991, wrote: 'Suicide is no longer an offence but properly considered as a manifestation of mental abnormality.'

Voluntary euthanasia is a form of suicide in that the person decides for himself or herself that life is no longer worth living and they would prefer to be dead. It is not surprising that most people assume, therefore, that voluntary euthanasia and religious belief cannot go together. As far as religious authorities and leaders go, this is, in the main, true. Voluntary euthanasia requires people to think for themselves about the end of their lives, decide for themselves and take responsibility for their actions. Very few religious sects respect the autonomy of the individual to this extent.

The major Christian church that allows the least decision-making to the ordinary individual is the Roman Catholic church. *Humanae Vitae*, the papal encyclical issued in 1968, states unequivocally:

> *Let no Catholic be heard to assert that the interpretation of the natural moral law is outside the competence of the church authorities. Jesus Christ, when he communicated his divine powers to Peter and the other apostles and sent them to teach all nations his commandments, constituted them as the authentic guardians and interpreters of the whole moral law, not only, that is, of the law of the gospel but also of the natural law, the reason being that the natural law declares the will of God, and its faithful observance is necessary for men's eternal salvation.*

In other words, the pope pronounces the doctrine, and Roman Catholics must obey or risk losing eternal salvation. This is the theory. What happens in practice we can see most easily in the case of contraception. The only form of family limitation approved by the Vatican is abstinence, yet Italy, nominally a Catholic country, has the lowest birth-rate in Europe. Are we to believe that this is achieved by sexual abstinence? Surely not.

Similarly, when it comes to voluntary euthanasia, papal edicts, which never use the word 'voluntary' in this context, categorically forbid it. Indeed, the Vatican's 1980 *Declaration on Euthanasia* says that 'suffering has a special place in God's saving plan'. In the Netherlands, where roughly one-third of the population call themselves Catholic, there is an overwhelming majority of the population who support its current availability there. A Dutch doctor commented: 'When a patient asks me for euthanasia I always ask if he would like to talk about it with a priest or humanist counsellor. If they ask for a priest I have never known one, Catholic or Protestant, to refuse. And if the patient wants that priest to be there when they die, that happens too.'

So, when we hear about the official doctrine of a particular religion, we should guard against assuming that this is how its members actually behave. Many, if not most, believers seem to find little difficulty in picking out the bits of the doctrine that they will observe in daily life and ignoring the rest. In the case of the Netherlands and voluntary euthanasia, this seems to apply to Catholic priests as well as to ordinary members of the congregation.

The conference at which the Protestant priest raised the question of our harsher treatment of a dying man than of a dying animal was entitled 'Controversies in the Care of the Dying Patient'. It was attended mainly by doctors and nurses, and it became clear that most participants felt it was time something was done about the practice of keeping patients alive indefinitely. It was held in the United States, which routinely goes further in this direction than any other country.

One of the speakers confronted the conference with a blunt description of the condition of an Alzheimer's patient: 'He's in diapers. The only sound he makes is a sort of animal grunting. He shows no sign of awareness of people or his surroundings.' This patient was a former dean of the medical school that had organized the conference.

Another speaker was Edmund Pellegrino, an eminent doctor, an authority on medical ethics and a devout Catholic. He said that while he could see the arguments in favour of allowing mercy killing, he would never be able to do it because of his religion. He was reminded that the Catholic church approves of war, provided that the pope pronounces it a 'just' war. Pellegrino's reply was: 'I have been a lifelong pacifist.' This man has written many books on medical ethics, always explicitly from a Roman Catholic point of view, yet he did not accept one of his church's basic tenets.

The individual Catholic who does not regard all papal doctrine as binding is not necessarily an internationally famous moral philosopher. The man in the street may be just as independent and as untroubled about the consequences. Catholics are in a small minority in Britain, although they form the majority of regular church-goers. In Germany some states are predominantly Catholic and some Protestant. In 1990 a survey of German Catholics showed that only 16 per cent of them were guided in their everyday lives by the pope's pro-nouncements. Four years later a similar survey carried out in predominantly Catholic France showed that 83 per cent of French citizens thought that they should go solely by their own consciences and only 1 per cent by the official teaching of the Catholic church.

The same 'pick-and-choose' attitude can be demonstrated in the series of five National Opinion Polls, which have been conducted in Britain since 1969. The same question has been put to the random sample of just over 2,000 adults on each occasion: 'Some people say that the law should allow adults to receive medical help to a peaceful death if they suffer from an incurable physical illness that is intolerable to them, provided they have previously requested such help in writing. Please tell me whether you agree or disagree with this.'

In 1969 only 50 per cent were in favour. By 1993 this had risen to 79 per cent, with only 10 per cent disagreeing; the rest were 'don't knows'. After replying, the respondents were asked about their religious belief. The results, in percentages of those in favour were: Humanists, atheists and agnostics (i.e., people with no religious belief) 93; Protestants 83; Roman Catholics 73; and Jews 60. Britain today is a predominantly secular society, with an extremely low rate of church atten-dance, but it is clear that even among those who do describe themselves as holding a particular religious belief there is a majority in favour of legalizing voluntary euthanasia. They ei-ther do not know or do not care that they are in opposition to their religious authorities.

In 1995 a professor of theology at the German University of Tübingen published a book called *A Dignified Dying*. Hans Kung is a Catholic. He accepts that the word 'euthanasia' should be used in its proper sense of 'good death', even in Germany, where the memory of its misuse by the Nazis is naturally more vivid than anywhere else. He draws attention to the fact that all those supporting the social acceptance of euthanasia insist that it must be voluntary and that strong controls are always included in laws allowing voluntary euthanasia.

Professor Kung describes the dreadful death of his 23-year-old brother from brain cancer. It happened when Professor Kung himself was a newly ordained Catholic priest, and the experience led to his continually questioning throughout his forty years of teaching and writing about Catholic doctrine whether such a death can be 'the will of God'. His conclusion is that, although he regards life as the gift of God, he regards it as a human task and responsibility. This dual approach means that he can accept contraception and medical aid in dying as the exercise of human responsibility, which takes into account individual circumstances.

The contrast between this eminent Catholic's view and official papal doctrine is stark. The most recent published ruling on correct Catholic behaviour, *Humanae Vitae*, concentrates on contraception, abortion and euthanasia. These are the very issues on which, for the benefit of society as a whole, consensus is most needed among believers in all religious faiths and those with no religious beliefs. Simply issuing absolute rulings against attempting a rational approach to these problems helps no one. A recent book, *Dilemmas of a Catholic Doctor*, concludes that: 'Ordinary people who by nature and nurture are close to the processes of life and death have a wisdom in these matters which has not been sufficiently acknowledged by moralists and theologians.'

Although the ordinary Catholic is almost as likely as everyone else to approve of voluntary euthanasia, spokespeople opposing it on television and radio, or in the press are nearly always Catholic. The only other group that provides speakers to argue against it are hospice doctors, and many of these base their arguments on religious grounds. This is true of Britain and the former Commonwealth countries. In North America, too, the most vociferous opposition to legalizing voluntary euthanasia comes from the Catholic church.

The commonest starting point for asserting that the Bible

forbids voluntary euthanasia is the commandment 'Thou shalt not kill'. It would, apparently, be more accurately translated as 'Thou shalt not murder', which is nearly, but not quite, the same. In both cases the word implies violence and crime, and more importantly, from the point of view of voluntary euthanasia and mercy killing, they imply that the victim has a life worth living and would much prefer not to be killed. Neither of these statements is true of a person who is so near the end of life that they are asking a doctor to help them to a peaceful death.

There are some people who say, 'If you end someone's life there's only one word for it, you kill them.' But the English language very rarely has only one word for a particular act. Consider the act of sexual penetration and ejaculation. It is usually love-making, but sometimes it is rape. There may be no way an observer could tell the difference, but the receiver of the act knows which it is, and it is whether that person wanted it that makes one acceptable and the other a crime. In the same way, we need one word for killing a healthy person against their will and a different word for bringing about the death of an incurably ill person who now wants only to die. The first can be accidental death, murder or manslaughter. Since there is no single separate word for the second we shall have to continue to use the phrase 'help to die'. 'Thou shalt not help to die' does not have the same unanswerable quality as 'Thou shalt not kill'. In fact, if I am a doctor and my dying patient is consistently asking me for this help, I may very well feel that this is the right thing to do. As a Dutch doctor put it: 'It is my last act of medical care for my autonomous patient.'

'Life is a gift from God, and only He can decide when it shall come to an end', is another common assertion made by people who do not want voluntary euthanasia to be legalized. To those people who do not believe there is a God, this statement is, of course, meaningless, but even those with a religious faith that postulates the existence of a single masculine transcendental being would not agree about what it means. It certainly seems to forbid contraception, yet the vast majority of Christians and Jews practise it. At the other end of life, many Christians feel that the doctors who are giving them life-preserving treatment are frustrating God's intentions.

Lord Soper is a former President of the Methodist Conference and also a vice-president of the British Voluntary Euthanasia Society. He says of his father: 'At the end of his life – and it was a very full and in many ways a saintly life – he complained somewhat bitterly to me that the doctors were hindering his approach to the celestial world to which he had looked forward for the whole of his life. He wanted to go home.'

A reflective comment from one reader on Lord Soper's words was: 'I'm sure my parents received their call from God several years ago, and in my opinion they were very foolish to turn it down.'

A leading Church of England cleric has argued strongly that suicide is morally acceptable when it benefits others as well as the sufferer, starting with Christ giving up his life for the sake of humanity. He cites the self-sacrifice of heroes and heroines throughout history and extends this to the present. Wanting not to impose an intolerable burden on one's children is often a contributory reason for choosing to die.

The inconsistency of the attitude shown by the medical profession towards patients' end-of-life decisions is nowhere more striking than in its attitude to Jehovah's Witnesses. On the basis of the biblical verses 'But flesh with the life therof, which is the blood thereof, shall ye not eat' (Genesis 9:4) and 'That ye abstain from meats offered to idols, and from blood, and from things strangled, and from fornication' (Acts 15:29) they refuse to accept blood transfusions. When the person dies whose life would have been saved by the transfusion, this is not regarded by them as suicide. To non-Jehovah's Witnesses the equating of receiving a blood transfusion with eating seems odd, and the fact that refusing the transfusion involves choosing to die seems to make it a suicidal decision. However, the British medical profession has always accepted this as a binding refusal when explicitly made by a competent adult. In 1992 a 24-year-old unconscious man was allowed to bleed to death after his wife produced a written statement from him saying that he was a Jehovah's Witness and refused blood transfusions. The surgeons were told that the health authority had forbidden the use of blood in these circumstances, although no doctor has ever been sued in Britain for giving a patient a blood transfusion against his will.

It is possible for doctors to have a child quickly made a Ward of Court if it is being refused a necessary blood transfusion by its parents, but it is not known whether this usually happens. In 1993 a father *was* jailed for two years for denying insulin injections to his nine-year-old diabetic daughter. He was found guilty of manslaughter, and the child's mother was given a suspended sentence. The parents were members of the Zion Ethiopian Church, whose followers believe in homeopathic medicine.

It is estimated that medical decisions bring forward or postpone about a third of deaths in the Netherlands, and there is no reason to think the figures would be substantially different wherever modern medicine is practised. These are decisions to refrain from or discontinue medical treatment that appears futile, and they are made by doctors, not by God. Doctors who could give further life-prolonging treatment to a patient but who decide not to do so sometimes use the expression, 'We have decided to let Nature take its course.' Opponents of active voluntary euthanasia often say 'doctors mustn't play God', meaning that they cannot interfere with God's plan and end a life. They seem unaware of the inconsistency of interfering with God's apparent plan by preventing the ending of a life. As one doctor put it: 'If by playing God they mean giving treatment without which the patient would die, then it is something that I and most doctors do several times a working day. Preventing Nature taking its course is a good description of the whole of medical practice.'

Many of the quotations and assertions referred to above are common to Christianity and Judaism. Among the groups who call themselves Christians, there is a wide spectrum of views about the fundamentals of good behaviour. There is a similar split between what the leaders say, especially the more dogmatic leaders, and what the majority of ordinary Jews think and do. Unlike the Catholic church, there is no one world figurehead in Judaism. The nearest thing to a worldwide consensus would be the opinion of the World Jewish Congress, and that body has taken no official stand on the issue of euthanasia.

The Jewish tradition is of intense argument on the interpretation of their sacred texts, and orthodox Jews contribute vigorously to the academic journals in which medical ethics are debated. They also attend and organize international conferences on the subject, in numbers out of all proportion to the size of the congregations whose views they represent. It would probably be fair to say that this body of religious opinion coincides on the question of euthanasia with that of the official Catholic position – that is, it accepts the right of the patient to refuse futile treatment in the face of incurable illness. It also accepts the so-called 'doctrine of double-effect', which is the belief that a doctor may increase the level of pain-killers to the point where the death will most probably be accelerated, *provided* that the doctor does not intend to cause the death.

That the doctor is, in effect, saying, 'I am killing the pain, not the patient', is a ruling that strikes many non-theologians as so ludicrous that they can scarcely believe that it is seriously propounded by leading churchmen. In fact, leaders of the medical profession frequently bring it forward with approval, too. Many people who would like the choice of a consciously chosen good death find the doctrine insulting for several reasons – the decision must be the doctor's, the result is uncertain and, finally, the death becomes a mere side-effect of the doctor's chosen treatment. While they are still rational and conscious, the patients would usually prefer their deaths to have rather more significance than that. Dying as a mere side-effect of someone else's action is not seen as a dignified death – even when the someone else is a doctor.

In summary, therefore, the official doctrines of the Roman Catholic church and of orthodox Judaism reject active euthanasia but accept all forms of passive euthanasia. On the whole, neither religion is much interested in the question of who decides; it appears to be assumed that the doctor will be the decision-maker. The other denominations within Christianity and Judaism are less outspoken and dogmatic in their official attitudes to individual choice in dying. They can be found in more detail in *Playing God* by Gerald Larue, which discusses the positions taken by the other major world religions on this question.

The people who write about medical ethics are, by training, mostly moral philosophers, but some are also doctors or lawyers. Some medical ethicists base their ideas on their religious faith, but not all of them point this out to the reader. This means that the rational arguments produced in their books and academic journals may or may not be resting on unspoken assumptions that are incapable of rational proof. Readers would be in a better position to weigh up the arguments if they knew the author's starting point. The idea that ethics – the study of moral principles – must have a religious connotation is still prevalent, even in these secular times. It is widely implied that those with no religious faith have no moral principles either, but from the age of classical Greece to modern times there have always been individual philosophers who do not base their arguments about ethics on religious belief. Among those writing today, one of the most eminent is Ronald Dworkin. In his book *Life's Dominion: an Argument about Abortion and Euthanasia*, he concludes that voluntary euthanasia should be a matter of choice by the individual: 'Making someone die in a way that others approve, but he believes a horrifying contradiction of his life, is a devastating, odious form of tyranny.'

A working party set up by the British Institute of Medical Ethics looked at the problem from the point of view of the doctor. Could it ever be morally acceptable for a doctor to respond to a patient's request for voluntary euthanasia? Its conclusion was:

A doctor, acting in good conscience, is ethically justified in assisting death if the need to relieve intense and unceasing pain or distress caused by an incurable illness greatly outweighs the benefit to the patient of further prolonging his life. This conclusion applies to patients whose sustained wishes on this matter are known to the doctor and should thus be respected as outweighing any contrary opinion expressed by others.

The importance of the attitudes of religious leaders to voluntary euthanasia does not rest on the fact that they influence the opinions of their nominal followers decisively. As we have seen, most followers of all religions make up their own minds on the basis of their life experiences. The pope, internationally, and the other religious spokesmen within their own countries acquire their importance precisely from the fact that they are spokesmen. In the media, especially on television, their opinions are given air-time as if they still spoke for the majority of the population. The members of the various parliaments also turn to them rather than to their constitutents for pronouncements on ethical matters.

The media is probably also misled by the size of the immense crowds that gather to see the pope on his world travels, although, of course, equally large crowds gather to see pop music and sport celebrities. Among these crowds there will, of course, be individuals who base their whole conduct in life on the rulings of the church. They will, however, be in a small minority, and the politicians in democracies would do well to take note of this fact.

7

How has the law forbidding voluntary euthanasia changed?

◇

Marshall Perron became more interested in voluntary euthanasia after a distressing death in his family. Nothing unusual in that, of course; it is one of the commonest reasons given by new members when they join one of the societies campaigning to make it a legal option. However, he happened to be chief minister of the Australian Northern Territory, so when he decided the law needed changing he was in a much stronger position to put his resolve into effect than an ordinary citizen. Any change in the law he proposed would, of course, have to be presented in his role as an ordinary MP. It would be voted on by MPs according to their own convictions, not necessarily according to their political party, and it would have to secure a majority in order to become law. Nevertheless, a chief minister commands a wider audience for his views than most people. He can expect a more prompt reply to his enquiries, and secretarial and research help is not likely to be lacking.

In area, Northern Territory is one of the bigger states of Australia, but in population it is much the smallest. Few people, even the resourceful Aboriginals, have ever managed to live in the hot, arid regions that make up most of it. Some of the traditional Aboriginals continue to live as they have always lived, or as much like that as is possible nowadays, but many have been assimilated into the multi-cultural society that is the norm in the modern developed world. There are 25 MPs in the legislature, in the capital city, Darwin.

At the time Marshall Perron became interested in the subject, there was no voluntary euthanasia society in Darwin. The state capitals Adelaide, Melbourne, Sydney and Perth all had societies campaigning for the legal right to choose a merciful death, so these societies were his first source of information when he started to find out how his relative could have been helped to an earlier death if she had desired it. The societies also had model Bills, which they were doing their best to present to the Parliaments of South Australia, Victoria, New South Wales and Western Australia, so he did not have to start from scratch. Even so, it was a remarkable achievement to have the Bill ready to present to the Darwin legislature within the year, in February 1995. Marshall Perron's problems then began, as the opposition, mainly from church organizations, sprang into action all over Australia.

Although the Irish who left Ireland following the potato famine in the middle of the nineteenth century went mainly to North America, considerable numbers made their new homes in Australia. So the Catholic church is strongly entrenched there. After the Second World War the new wave of immigrants came largely from southern Europe. Athens, for example, is the only city that has a larger Greek population than Melbourne, and the conflict in the former Yugoslavia must have caused much heartache among the considerable numbers of Yugoslavs who emigrated to Australia. Although these new communities have brought their religious customs with them, there is much variety among those religious affiliations. Groups aimed at preventing their own language, music, songs, dancing and traditional costumes from being forgotten often focus on a church.

These two population groups probably provide the most support for the church-led opposition to legalizing voluntary euthanasia, although 77 per cent of Australians say they have some form of religious faith. Despite this, 81 per cent of Australians support the choice of voluntary euthanasia being available towards the end of life. In most respects, Australia is a secular society with a sturdy tradition of looking problems straight in the eye and tackling them on the basis of individual conviction.

In his speech presenting his Bill for its second reading, Marshall Perron described the campaign against the Bill by the Australian Medical Association and the right-to-life groups as dishonest and he added: 'Whoever told traditional Aboriginals that we will round sick people up and end their lives, ought to be ashamed of themselves.' This allegation has not been made in print in Britain, but one of the right-to-life spokespersons had said: 'How typical of them to start in a state where most of the people are Aboriginals who won't understand what's going on!' She probably knew as little about Aboriginals as she did about the circumstances of the origin of this Bill. One crucial speech in passing the Rights of the Terminally Ill Act was actually made by an Aboriginal MP, Wes Lanhupuy, who quoted the 'totally devastating' death of his wife from cancer.

Some of the provisions included in this first law permitting active voluntary euthanasia are shown in the summary opposite. The elaborate parliamentary–legal language in which laws have to be framed has been omitted from this summary of the Act, which came into effect on 1 July 1996.

Sir Ernest Titterton was an Australian nuclear scientist who died in 1990. Three years earlier, at the age of 70, he became paralysed from the neck down following a car accident. In a taped message to a Medical Conference on Brain Injuries he said: 'If euthanasia were legal I should opt for it tomorrow. In fact, I would have opted for it two years ago.'

**Rights of the Terminally Ill Act 1995
Legislative Assembly of the Northern Territory**

The Act confirms the right of a terminally ill person to request assistance from a medically qualified person to voluntarily terminate his or her life in a humane manner.

- The patient must be over 18 and terminally ill.

- Assistance may be by administering appropriate drugs or supplying them for the patient to self-administer.

- The illness must be causing severe pain/suffering.

- The patient must not be suffering from treatable depression (an independent psychologist must confirm this).

- The doctor must share the same first language as the patient or have an accredited translator present.

- The patient must be offered and must positively refuse all further palliative care.

- There must be a period for reflection between the first discussions and the final decision.

- The doctor must be present until the patient has died.

- Insurance will not be affected.

- Foreigners will not be able to travel to Australia to benefit by the Act. (Immigration laws bar visitors in poor health.)

That it should be an Australian legislature to achieve the world first in change in statute law to allow doctor-assisted death for the incurably ill at their considered request has been a surprise. For a long time it looked as though it would be the Netherlands that took that step, and then Oregon, in the United States, looked as though it had some claim to that position. The Dutch Parliament has not yet framed a law to legalize the careful practice of voluntary euthanasia. The Netherlands Criminal Code actually says:

> *Anyone who takes the life of another at that other's express and serious request, will be punished with a prison sentence of a maximum of twelve years [and] anyone who deliberately incites another to commit suicide, assists him in so doing or provides the means for him to do so will, if suicide follows, be punished with a prison sentence of a maximum of three years.*

In effect, both active voluntary euthanasia and assisted suicide are illegal in the Netherlands. But note what a difference three words can make. 'If suicide follows' is not part of the 1961 British Act forbidding assisted suicide. Only two people have been given prison sentences under this Act, and one of them was convicted on the basis of a secretly recorded conversation with her mother, who afterwards did not even attempt suicide, let alone succeed.

However, statute law – meaning law made by a Parliament – is not the only source of law. The result of one trial in court can establish 'case law', and if later cases rest on the same legal principle, the judgement given in the first one will be used. Although the expression 'case law' is not used in the Netherlands, the system of referring to earlier judgements is quite similar. In 1978 a Dutch court trying Mrs Wertheim, who was accused of aiding a suicide, said: 'The law rightly tries to prevent suicide as much as possible. However, in exceptional circumstances someone's decision to end his life must be respected. Assisting him to do so in a humane manner is in those circumstances not a crime in the opinion of the court.'

In 1973 Dr Postma ended the life of her mother, who was over 90 years old, incurably ill and expressing her wish to die (she was herself a doctor, as it happens). Dr Postma reported what she had done and was charged with breaking the Dutch penal code. It was judged that she was in an impossible position because, as a doctor, she had a duty to act in the best interest of her patient and in this case that conflicted with her duty, like that of any other citizen, not to break the law. The court held that in giving voluntary euthanasia, a doctor was letting the first duty override the second, and this was appropriate when no other medical means existed for ending the patient's suffering.

There have been over 20 court cases since then, each raising slightly different aspects of the various circumstances and medical decisions. Every death is unique, after all, even if all deaths have many features in common. In 1984 the Dutch Medical Association published the criteria to be observed by a doctor who decides to respond to his or her patient's request for help to die. These are:

1. Voluntary and durable request

2. Full information

3. Unacceptable and hopeless suffering

4. No acceptable alternatives left

5. Consultation with another physician.

Dutch doctors who help a patient to die, even when they know they have carefully observed the above guidelines, still have to report what they have done to the prosecuting authorities because it is still technically a criminal act. It can then be weeks or even months before they hear whether the Public Prosecutor has decided to send the case to trial, just to make sure. If there is to be a trial, there are months of waiting – in a recent case it was three years – before it comes to court. Small wonder that they sometimes report the death as the natural one that it would have been without their merciful intervention. The Dutch government did not like not knowing what was happening, and in 1990 the Medical Association and the Ministry of Justice agreed on a formal notification procedure, which reassured doctors about their position. This has influenced doctors' willingness to report cases of voluntary euthanasia and the number of reports has increased from 454 in 1990 to 1,323 in 1992.

These developments in the Netherlands have aroused great interest in the rest of the world. Hostile, inaccurate and prejudiced reports have abounded and have been published in otherwise reputable newspapers and journals. The worst of these was probably that of the major American medical ethics journal, *The Hastings Center Report*, which published a special supplement on the subject in January 1989. It included all sorts of unsupported allegations of shocking practices in the Netherlands. The Dutch Health Council and Dutch Medical Association immediately wrote setting the record straight, but it was December 1989 before they were published, and even then no apology was forthcoming.

One assertion frequently made by those who do not want the rest of us to have the choice of medical help in dying is that the Dutch have voluntary euthanasia because they have no hospice care of the dying. In fact, the Dutch have excellent hospice care, although there are no special buildings called hospices. Nurses trained in palliative care of the dying do most of their work in patients' own homes or in the nursing homes where the patients live. Increasing numbers of hospice-trained nurses work in the community in Britain, too.

In the face of this kind of foreign misrepresentation and also for its own better information, the Dutch government commissioned a wide-ranging study of death and dying throughout the Netherlands. This report was published in 1991, and it remains unique in its scale and thoroughness. Comparable reliable facts and figures are not available for any other country. It is known as the Remmelink Report, after its chairman, Professor Remmelink. In many ways the most interesting statistic to emerge from this study is that over a third of deaths, 35 per cent, follow a medical decision that may hasten the death. Half of these decisions are to discontinue, or not to start, treatment that would prolong the patient's life. The other half follow the treatment of distressing symptoms by high dosages of opioids. There is no reason to think the figures would be substantially different for Britain, where both these practices happen legally. In neither country is the patient's consent required for this treatment.

The Remmelink Report found that 0.8 per cent of deaths had been brought about by doctors' life-terminating acts without the conditions for voluntary euthanasia being fulfilled. A further study of these was undertaken, and it was found that nearly all these patients were suffering great distress and were within hours of death anyway. It was also found that their doctors had known them and their wishes for many years, and further that many of them were in the process of completing their voluntary euthanasia arrangements when their condition deteriorated to the point where action was necessary.

The following death was of this kind. It happened in a major London teaching hospital. 'We can't allow him to go on suffering like this,' the doctors said, as Edmund fought for breath. The cancerous growth that was closing his windpipe had already closed his throat, and the cancer was widely spread throughout the rest of his body.

'Oh, please wait until our sons get here!' This was Edmund's wife speaking.

'Would you really want them to see him like this?' was the reply.

She realized how inhumane her reaction had been, and Edmund was given the drugs that brought his terminal suffering to a merciful end.

There is no reason to think that such crises occur more or less frequently wherever modern medicine is practised, and merciful doctors take the appropriate action, as the royal physician Lord Dawson said in 1935, opposing a law to allow voluntary euthanasia, 'All good doctors do it anyway'. The difference between the Netherlands and all other countries, is that figures are available for how often Dutch doctors do it.

The 'unacceptable and hopeless suffering' referred to in the guidelines has always been taken to mean physical suffering, although the emotional suffering associated with the patient's condition has not been ignored. But in 1991 a patient, Mrs B, was helped to die although she was not physically ill.

Five years earlier her eldest son had committed suicide. He was 20 years old. Her marriage was breaking down at the same time, and she received psychiatric treatment, being herself strongly suicidal. Finally, she overcame this wish because she realized that her other son, who was 15 years old, needed her. Then he, in turn, died when he was 20, in his case of cancer, and during his final illness Mrs B had already decided that his death would be the end for her, too. She tried to commit suicide but failed. She asked the Dutch Voluntary Euthanasia Society for help and was referred to Dr Chabot, a psychiatrist. After 30 sessions of therapy, during which he failed to persuade her to accept anti-depressant drugs, he agreed to cooperate in her suicide. He said in a later interview: 'I did not agree with her decision to kill herself, but I felt that the greater evil would be her dying alone.' He prescribed the appropriate pills, was with her when she swallowed them and remained with her until she died. He then reported his role in her death to the authorities. This was not euthanasia because he did not administer the drugs. It was assisted suicide and, as such, illegal. The local court and the appeal court acquitted him, and although the Supreme Court ruled that he was guilty of breaking the law, it imposed no punishment.

Another recent case that was not voluntary euthanasia concerned a grossly handicapped baby. The parents and doctors together decided that the infant's outlook was so hopeless that it would be kinder to allow him to die. These decisions are frequently made in most countries, and when it happens in the United Kingdom the baby is given sedative drugs until it dies of lack of food. This seems cruel to many nurses and parents, and the Dutch doctor used drugs so that the baby died peacefully in its mother's arms within an hour, instead of over some days.

Recently the first case of discontinuing the life-support of a patient in a persistent vegetative state occurred in the Netherlands. This, again, is not voluntary euthanasia because the patient is past the point of being able to choose. When the Dutch frame a statute law about medical aid in dying, perhaps it will be confined to voluntary euthanasia. Perhaps it will set out the conditions for the proper practice of assisted suicide and for dealing with PVS patients and grossly handicapped babies as well. We shall see.

Meanwhile, on the other side of the Atlantic, things have developed differently. Although there has been a lot of case law, it has almost all, in the United States at any rate, been in the field of allowing patients to die, not helping them to die. First, Karen Quinlan was allowed to be taken off a ventilator, and she proved able to breathe enough to go on, with round-the-clock, one-to-one nursing, in her persistent vegetative state for another ten years. Then Nancy Cruzan's tube-feeding was allowed to be discontinued, and she died some days later. Quadriplegic young men have been allowed to come off their ventilators and have been given drugs to ease their dying. These are voluntary, chosen deaths, but because the doctors do not cause their death by administering drugs to stop their hearts, the law apparently accepts this as a form of suicide.

Dr Kevorkian has evaded several attempts by the Michigan authorities to stop him helping patients to die. On over forty occasions he has positively helped suffering patients to end their own lives in a painless and foolproof way. Most of these deaths have taken place in a caravan, because when he tried to rent a room in a hotel or take a temporary lease of a flat, he always explained why it was wanted. He was then turned away. Critics of Dr Kevorkian say that another doctor should be involved, there should be checks to be sure the patient is not suffering from treatable depression, and so on. His reply is that he would prefer those arrangements, but in the meantime, people are suffering from their inability to end their lives without help, and he seems to be the only one who will help them. An editorial in the *British Medical Journal* of 8 June 1996 described Dr Kevorkian as a hero because of his willingness to challenge the conservatism of the medical profession and the rigours of the law. In addition to providing the much-desired boon of a peaceful death to those forty-odd people, Dr Kevorkian has stimulated discussion of physician-assisted death in the United States. Progress in formulating the safeguards for its decriminalization is slow, but will be achieved, eventually. Six other Michigan doctors have formed a group called Physicians for Mercy, which aims for merciful, dignified, medically assisted termination of life under appropriate circumstances.

On the west coast matters have taken a different turn. Washington State, on the Pacific coast just south of Canada, is one of the 21 states in the United States whose constitution includes a Citizens' Initiative Procedure. This means that a group of ordinary people can frame a law and that at the next election everyone can vote for or against this law. It is the same as a referendum, but organized by citizens, not by the government, and, unlike a referendum, it becomes part of the law of the state – or should do – if it is approved by the electorate.

In 1990 a group of campaigners, calling themselves Death with Dignity, began collecting the 150,000 signatures they needed to frame a law under the Citizens' Initiative Procedure. Two years before, a similar group had tried the same process in California, but, with that state's bigger population, they had to collect many more signatures and narrowly failed to reach their target. In Washington State they collected 70,000 more than they needed, and all the polls in the months preceding the voting showed a majority in favour.

Then the opposition started showing emotive advertising, in particular suggesting that poor people would start asking for help to die to save their family's money in caring for them. It was suggested that the state would become filled with 'death clinics' as people flocked in from all over the United States to be helped to die. The voting turned out to be 54 per cent against and 46 per cent in favour, which was a great disappointment to all those in the state who had hoped to be able to get medical help to die well, if that proved to be necessary. The Attorney-General of Washington State filed a suit for 'false advertising' during the campaign, against the main opposition group, which included senior workers for the state's Catholic bishops.

In 1993 the Californian campaigners tried again, and this time they succeeded in gathering the 300,000 signatures they needed. But the measure was defeated by exactly the same margin as in Washington State, and it was defeated by the same well-funded, misleading advertising in the weeks before the voting. Most of the money for this was raised by Catholic organizations, although this was never mentioned in the advertisements.

The following year Oregon became the third of the west-coast states to tackle the problem of patient choice in dying through the initiative process. Learning from the experience of California and Washington State, campaigners succeeded – just – in fighting off effects of a well-funded TV campaign in the weeks before the voting took place. The voting was 51 per cent in favour, with 49 per cent against. Although this measure was acclaimed at the time as the first statute law to make voluntary euthanasia legal, it only gives the doctor the legal right to prescribe the necessary drugs for the patient to take independently. The doctor may not give them by injection. In effect, it legalizes doctor-assisted suicide. Moreover, unlike the Northern Territory's Act, which came into effect almost at once, the Oregon law was immediately blocked by the opponents' legal actions. A district judge ruled that the law is unconstitutional, but campaigners appealed to the Circuit Court of Appeals, and the losers in that court will probably appeal to the United States Supreme Court. There is a long way to go before this particular law comes into effect.

Meanwhile matters were going ahead in Washington State, which had a law making it a criminal act for a doctor to assist in the suicide of a terminally ill patient. With the help of a Seattle-based group, Compassion in Dying, three terminally ill patients and four doctors who care for the terminally ill challenged this law in the courts. 'Jane Roe' was 69 years old and had been a cancer patient about twenty years. By this time it was widespread through her bones, so any movement caused intense pain. Her medical and nursing care were excellent, and she was still mentally alert. Being a doctor herself, she thoroughly understood her condition, and her family sympathized with her wish to hasten her death, but she was prevented by law from honestly discussing this with her doctor.

The second patient, 'John Doe', was an AIDS patient, aged 44. His partner had died of AIDS in 1991, so he was vividly aware of how extreme his suffering was likely to be in the last few months of his life. He knew that his doctor would be committing a crime if he prescribed the drugs that would hasten his death, but he would prefer not to die by starvation and dehydration, his only alternative in the existing state of the law.

The third patient, 'James Poe', was a 69-year-old, who was dying of emphysema, an irreversible lung disease causing ever-decreasing ability to absorb enough oxygen. He used a tube connected to an oxygen tank 24 hours a day and, even so, suffered panic attacks when he felt he was suffocating. His family accepted his wish to hasten his death but did not know which drugs would bring about a peaceful death, nor in what quantities, nor how they should be given. And even if they did, they would need a doctor's prescription to get them.

The claim of these three patients, supported by four Washington State doctors, was that the law prohibiting assistance with suicide, as applied to doctors prescribing medications for mentally competent terminally ill adult patients who seek to hasten inevitable death, was unconstitutional. In 1996, by which time all three patients were dead, a Federal Appeals Court of eleven judges ruled in their favour, by a majority of eight to three, declaring that the Washington State law did indeed violate the United States Constitution. The written judgement explaining the decision says:

A competent terminally ill adult, having lived nearly the full measure of his life, has a strong liberty interest in choosing a dignified and humane death rather than being reduced at the end of his existence to a childlike state of helplessness, diapered, sedated, incontinent. How a person dies not only determines the nature of the final period of existence, but in many cases, the enduring memories held by those who love him.

The judgement applies to the states of Alaska, Washington, Oregon, Montana, Idaho, California, Nevada, Arizona and Hawaii.

A similar case in New York has had the same outcome. Another Federal Appeals Court was asked to rule that the assisted suicide law was unconstitutional, and it has done so. This ruling applies to the states of New York, Connecticut and Vermont. It is interesting that the judgement in this case was based on the discriminatory nature of the law, which allowed the option of suicide to those physically able to accomplish it but denied that option to those who could not do it unaided.

Either of these judgements may yet be appealed against in the United States Supreme Court.

In Canada, too, there have been legal decisions that recognize the patient's right to refuse life-sustaining treatment. In 1991, for example, a Quebec court granted the right of an incurably ill woman, aged 24, to be disconnected from a life-support system. Two years later a Canadian woman, Sue Rodriguez, appealed to the courts of British Columbia and finally to the Canadian Supreme Court, claiming that the law against doctor-assisted death was unconstitutional. That court ruled five to four against her, on the grounds that the state's interest in protecting life's sanctity takes precedence over the right to a dignified death. She suffered from amyotrophic lateral sclerosis (ALS), which is also known as Lou Gehrig's disease. As she grew increasingly helpless her husband and nine-year-old son set up a separate home, because she was anxious that her son should not be involved too closely in seeing her waste away. A few months later she said goodbye to them during a last visit. When they had left she died with the help of an unnamed doctor and in the presence of a close friend who was also a Canadian MP. The immense amount of publicity caused by her courageous struggle has stimulated great public interest in changing the law.

Annie Lindsell, at present suffering from a similar degenerative disease, is equally anxious to determine for herself the point at which she wants to deteriorate no further. Unfortunately, being British, there is no written constitution that she can allege is being breached by the fact that doctors are not allowed to help her.

In both Australia and the United States there are other states than those so far mentioned where repeated attempts are being made to introduce a law allowing the incurably ill and suffering patient to choose a dignified death. On the whole, the Australian states aim for voluntary euthanasia (the doctor may inject the appropriate drugs), while in the United States doctor-assisted suicide (the doctor only prescribes the drugs) is the preferred option. In New Hampshire three Death with Dignity Bills have been brought before the state legislature within five years, and each time one is defeated the publicity leads to more voters supporting voluntary euthanasia.

English common law is the basis of law in the United States and in Commonwealth countries. It takes no account of the motive of the person who deliberately ends a human life, nor do the suffering of the dying person and the fact they are asking for help to die make any difference. The act remains homicide. The only way to avoid a verdict of life imprisonment is by pleading 'diminished responsibility'. Many relatives who have been driven to mercy killing find this insulting and ridiculous. At the time when they finally helped their loved one, the act was the most seriously and carefully considered thing they had ever done.

In many other countries the law is different. The Italian, Spanish, German, Polish, Japanese, Swiss and Norwegian penal codes, for example, all allow a lighter sentence if the killing is carried out at the request of the dying person. Uruguay is unique. There, judges are allowed to withhold all punishment if a defendant, whose previous life has been honourable, commits a homicide motivated by compassion and induced by repeated requests of the victim.

In Germany and Switzerland assisting a suicide is not a crime, as long as the helper does not benefit under the terms of the dying person's will. Both these countries have very large voluntary euthanasia societies, and in German-speaking Switzerland especially, great advantage has been taken of this possibility for helping the terminally ill. Two famous novelists, one American but having lived in Switzerland for many years, chose to die with this help. The other, dying of cancer, was described as the Barbara Cartland of German popular fiction.

When he was 25 years old a Spanish ship's engineer was on holiday and broke his spine in a diving accident. Doctors gave him another five years of life at most. Twenty-six years later he asked the Spanish association Derecho a Morir Dignamente (Right to Die with Dignity) to help him apply to the courts. He wanted his doctors to allow him to die painlessly, without breaking the law. 'I feel like a head stuck on to a dead body,' he says. He is living with his 87-year-old father and his brother and sister-in-law. The Spanish constitution enshrines the rights of 'liberty, dignity and the development of the personality', and this formed the basis of his appeal. The court's decision was that it was unable to decide because: 'It is not a duty of the courts to replace or fill the voids or omissions of the Spanish legal system.' Ramón intends to appeal to the Spanish superior Court of Justice and, if necessary, to the European Court of Human Rights. Catholic traditions weigh heavily with the leaders of the Spanish legal and medical professions, but recent polls show that 66 per cent of the Spanish population think that the right to a dignified death should get legal recognition.

In China in 1995 Liu Shabo helped his terminally ill wife to commit suicide and was sentenced to three years' imprisonment. Following this the National Peoples' Congress began studying a motion to legalize voluntary euthanasia. At almost the same time the Yokohama District Court in Japan pronounced four conditions under which a doctor would be allowed to perform a mercy killing. These are that: the patient must be suffering unbearable physical pain; death must be inevitable and imminent; all possible alleviating treatments must have been given; and the patient must clearly express approval of shortening of life. Dr Mashohito Tokunaga, who gave a lethal injection to a terminally ill cancer patient, received a two-year suspended sentence. The judge said he did not follow these conditions.

The Japanese Society for Dying with Dignity found in 1994 that doctors had abided by the living wills of nearly all its members who died that year (273 cases out of 283).

Scottish law differs from that of the rest of the United Kingdom in some respects, notably in respect of assisted suicide. Committing suicide was never a crime in Scotland, so its decriminalization by the British Parliament in 1961 was inmaterial. As we have already noted, the Scottish members of the voluntary euthanasia movement formed a separate society and continued to publish guidance on the most effective means of committing suicide. It was thought that in England and Wales the publishers of such a handbook might be prosecuted for assisting a suicide.

In the United Kingdom as a whole there have been several attempts to introduce a Voluntary Euthanasia Bill into Parliament, so far without success. However there has been progress in recent years in case law involving decisions about incompetent patients, rather than voluntary choices made by the patient. The best known concerned a young man called Tony Bland who had suffered such massive and irreversible brain damage that he was no longer aware of anything. Permission was given by the court to remove his feeding tube and he died a few days later. That was in 1992.

In the following year the Court of Appeal ruled that doctors need not re-insert a disconnected feeding tube that was keeping a 24-year-old drug overdose victim alive, and the year after that the High Court decided that the 28-year-old victim of a heart attack after a motor-cycle accident should be allowed to die. In that case there was disagreement among the relatives, and the judgement was in the favour of the next-of-kin, in that case the wife.

It is interesting to note that the first case was appealed to the Court of Appeal and the House of Lords, the second to the Court of Appeal, and the third was regarded as settled at the High Court.

In 1996 in Scotland a similar case to Tony Bland's occurred – the patient had been in PVS for four years – and the decision to allow doctors to discontinue artificial feeding was the same.

There have been some cases involving the refusal of treatment on religious grounds. In 1992 a 24-year-old man was allowed to bleed to death after his wife produced a written statement from him saying that he was a Jehovah's Witness and would not accept blood transfusion. The surgeons were told that the health authority had forbidden the use of blood in these circumstances, although no doctor has ever been sued in Britain for giving a patient a blood transfusion against his will. Soon afterwards, there was a case involving a pregnant woman aged 20, who was injured in a road accident. She went into labour and needed a caesarean section. She told the hospital staff that she was a Jehovah's Witness and was not to be given blood. After the operation she became unconscious but was given blood because her father, who was not a Jehovah's Witness, obtained a High Court order directing the doctors to do this.

At about the same time the High Court authorized the force-feeding of a 37-year-old woman who was suffering from anorexia nervosa, but this decision was quashed by the Appeal Court. The High Court decision had given permission to overrule the patient's autonomy in order to preserve her life, but the Appeal Court reinstated the individual's right to make personal decisions. In this it had acted in accordance with the House of Lords judgement on the Tony Bland case, which held that when the principle of autonomy is in conflict with the principle of the sanctity of life, English law gives priority to autonomy.

In 1993 a very important judgement established the binding nature of advance directives. The case concerned a 68-year-old man who had intermittent bouts of mental illness. Surgeons predicted that he would die unless his gangrenous leg was amputated, and when he refused to consent to the operation a High Court judge travelled to the hospital to talk to him. The judge said he was satisfied that the man understood his prognosis and affirmed the patient's right to refuse treatment in these circumstances, saying that that right extended into any future time of incompetence.

In the Republic of Ireland in 1995 the Supreme Court ruled that the tube-feeding of a woman who had been in a coma for 23 years should be discontinued. The reasons given were that the tube-feeding was intrusive and constituted an interference with the integrity of her body. It could not be regarded as a normal means of nourishment. 'Her right to life necessarily implied the right to die a natural death,' continued the judge. 'The true cause of her death would not be the withdrawal of nourishment but the injuries she received in 1972.'

Despite this steady progress in the recognition of the careful practice of passive euthanasia by the courts, Britain is lagging behind the Netherlands, Australia and the United States in admitting that more than that is necessary. Opponents of law reform ignore the many cases where the present 'system' breaks down. One of the worst instances in recent years, although it attracted very little publicity, was of a man who was found guilty of murder. His crime was the mercy killing of his wife. (The case is described in Chapter 5.) At that time a Select Committee of the House of Lords was studying murder and life imprisonment. It recommended that murderers should not automatically be given life sentences but that the judge in each case should have discretion over the length of sentence. The Committee recommended no change on mercy killing – it would be unnecessary when the judge could give a merciful sentence. Unfortunately, the Committee did not say what it thought should happen if the government did not accept its recommendation. The government did not accept the Committee's recommendation, and the mandatory life sentence for murder remains in force.

Three years later there was a mercy killing that *did* hit the headlines. A doctor had ended the life of a grievously suffering patient, a woman he had been treating for 13 years who had repeatedly asked him to see that her death was not distressing. The doctor took the unusual step of recording precisely what he had done in the patient's hospital notes. A senior nurse, also unusually, reported this to the hospital management team, which reported it to the police. The nurse in question was a Catholic, although she claimed this had nothing to do with her decision. The doctor was charged with attempted murder, but it was widely believed that the prosecution would not be proceeded with – a similar case had been dropped a few years earlier. When this did not happen, however, few people expected the jury to find him guilty, but it did, although many of the jurors were in tears as they did so. The sentence was one of probation, and the General Medical

Council did not strike the doctor off the medical register.

The case caused a public outcry. There were editorials in the major newspapers, and both leading medical journals called for reform of the law to cover such cases. Another House of Lords Select Committee was established, this time to look at medical ethics. In fact, although a great many other topics fall within the scope of medical ethics, the Committee considered only passive and active euthanasia. Its report recognized the competent patient's right to refuse treatment, both at the time and in advance, by means of an advance directive. A doctor could give pain-killers in such quantities that the patient's life was shortened, provided that the death was not intended, but the Committee recommended that it should remain a crime to end a life intentionally, no matter what the patient's sufferings and wishes.

This failure to suggest any means by which the law could be brought more into line with the overwhelming weight of public opinion led Ian Kennedy, Professor of Law and Medical Ethics at London University, to the view that Britain will now proceed by the gradual acceptance in the courts of changes in medical practice, as has happened in the Netherlands.

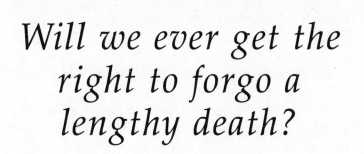

8

Will we ever get the right to forgo a lengthy death?

◇

One-third of the deaths recorded in the Remmelink Report, the Dutch report on death and dying, involved medical decisions towards the end of life (MDEL), which were pro-death decisions. These decisions were not about the giving of drugs that brought about the death; they were decisions not to give at all, or to stop giving, treatments that would have enabled the patient to go on living. A dramatic example is not to give resuscitation when the heart stops beating; another positive decision not to hinder any further an approaching death is to abstain from giving the antibiotics that would cure pneumonia if it develops. But there are many less direct ways of contributing to an earlier death.

'I'm not sending her to the acute hospital this time. I've no doubt they could patch her up enough to come home, ready for her next stroke,' the doctor told the patient's husband.

'No. She said last time she didn't want to go there again.'

Two days after her admission to the community hospital, the husband saw the doctor. 'She seems a bit better and she wants to come home.'

'I'd rather keep her in over the weekend.' The doctor knew that the 85-year-old husband was approaching exhaustion, and he probably also realized that with the one-to-one nursing that she got at home the wife spent more time sitting up and out of bed (which meant there was less chance of developing pneumonia).

On Monday the doctor saw the husband again. 'I'm afraid she has pneumonia. I think we should now just let nature take its course. Do you think she wanted to go on struggling?'

'No. I don't think she did.'

This 82-year-old lady had had innumerable small strokes, each leaving her slightly more disabled. The medical means to prevent her death were available, but they were not used. Her consent to this was assumed, almost certainly correctly.

We have no figures for the frequency of this kind of happening, except the Dutch ones, but medical practice is broadly similar in the industrially developed nations, and the process described above is perfectly acceptable everywhere. It is called 'avoiding futile treatment'. Sometimes the ironically intended words of Arthur Hugh Clough are quoted:

> *Thou shalt not kill; but needst not strive*
> *Officiously to keep alive.*

The fact that there are no publicly known or accepted guidelines for its practice or for recording its frequency means that there is also no telling how often and to what extent the patient is consulted. The opponents of legalizing voluntary euthanasia talk a great deal about its dangers because of possible abuse. They seem unconcerned about this sort of 'allowing to die', which used to be called passive euthanasia, and its possible abuse.

Whether it occurs with or without the involvement of the

patient in the decision-making process, the forgoing of available medical treatment towards the end of life is now a widespread practice and one that will certainly increase. There are many reasons for this.

The last fifty years have seen everyone's way of life change in previously unthinkable ways. Many of the changes that have occurred have contributed to the fact that the population everywhere includes a higher proportion of old people than it used to – a process usually called the 'ageing of the population'. The expectation of life has risen dramatically, and the biblical 'threescore years and ten' is now the average length of life, even in the less developed parts of the world. In the industrialized nations as a whole we can expect to live to be nearly 80 and in Japan, in particular, still older.

Medical advances spring to mind as the first cause of this phenomenon, and it is true that they have played a major part. Modern drugs have enabled previously fatal diseases to be cured, and all kinds of medical techniques restore our health in ways hitherto undreamed of. The control, and in some cases elimination, of many of the major infectious diseases by inoculation and vaccination has transformed the survival rates of children. As this realization becomes a fact of life, the birthrate has begun to fall in countries where previously the only way of providing for one's care in old age lay in being survived by at least one child. This can be seen already, for example, in Bangladesh. The fact that fewer children are born contributes still more to the predominance of the elderly.

The average standard of living all over the world has increased, however patchily. Of course, the contrast remains between the wealth and wastefulness of the industrially advanced nations and the lives of most in the rest of the world. Nevertheless, advances in the types of food crops grown, for example, means that few now go hungry. A rising standard of living contributes both to individuals living longer and to people limiting the size of their families. The one or two children in a family are confidently expected to survive, and the intention is to give them better life opportunities than the parents could afford for more children. The fact that women, for a variety of reasons, now expect to form part of the working population outside the home also tends to limit family size. Throughout Europe, except for Scandinavia, there has been a steady decline in the birth-rate over the last 20 years. Italy and Ireland, which had traditions of large families, have both had a sudden drop in the size of the average family size in the last ten years.

There are many consequences of this ageing of the population. Most of these consequences will need flexibility and willingness for change if all is to go smoothly. For example, in Britain at the age of 65 a working man used to stop working and begin to draw on savings accumulated collectively during his working life, in the form of a state pension. This was all very well when, on average, he died when he reached the age of 70. Now that he is likely to live until he is almost 80, it is a different story.

It is, in fact, relatively easy for a society with a high standard of living to make sure that retired people have enough to live on without undue hardship. There are plenty of useful activities available for men and women to busy themselves with in the early years of retirement, and the thrifty ones among them use some of their savings to travel the world, visiting their scattered relatives or as tourists and providing quite congenial work for armies of younger people in the process.

More serious problems arise with the advancing years. From the age of 80 on the proportion of people who can no longer manage the activities of daily living unaided begins to rise, and it rises steeply. It is this seventh stage of life that will bring about the most fundamental changes in our practices, laws and attitudes. This is partly because of the very advances in medical knowledge and techniques that are such a blessing to us all, as long as they improve our quality of life. Unfortunately, these same advances can also be used to keep alive people who are past the point of regaining their health. Some of those who are prevented, by the use of modern medicine, from dying of incurable conditions are young – many of those in the later stages of AIDS and most quadriplegics, for example – but most are old. If every possible means were to be used to maintain the failing lives of all of them, the health resources of even the richest states would be overwhelmed. The plain fact is that it has become impossible to maintain the lives of all the dependent elderly to the maximum. Or, as one doctor has put it: 'No country can now give state of the art medical care to all its citizens.'

There are many examples of this process of rationing having already begun. In the United States, for instance, health institutions that depend on public funding must establish their patients' end-of-life preferences when they are admitted. The reasons given for this change in the law were, it was said, so that patients could be treated in accordance with their own wishes and to avoid futile treatment. The fact remains, however, that up to that point it was the general practice to use all life-prolonging measures to the maximum extent. At that time, half the Medicare budget was being spent on the last few months of life.

In Britain a study published in *The Lancet* in 1995 showed that old people with lung cancer were not being given chemotherapy treatment to the same extent as young people. This was despite the fact that they responded equally well to the treatment, which reduced their symptoms as well as extending their lives. The Medical Research Council published findings in 1994 showing that doctors tend to assume too much that age in itself should be a determining factor in deciding to offer some treatments, an assumption that does not recognize the great variability in health of old people.

The following year central government ordered several health authorities to reverse spending cuts previously made in the provision of services for the elderly, the long-term sick and the terminally ill. There is pressure for a more uniform standard throughout the country in the provision of long-term care of the elderly and the chronically ill, but central government is resisting this 'to allow flexibility to cater for local needs'. The government avoids acknowledging that nationally there must be rationing of these provisions. But the facts reveal a rather different picture.

The dialysis statistics for both Britain and for Spain show a sharp falling off for patients at the age of 55, in marked contrast to the rest of Europe. In Britain at any rate, there has never been any publicity given to this policy, if, indeed, it is a national policy. If it is not, it seems a remarkable coincidence that so many renal departments have the same age-limit. In 1995 a 77-year-old New Zealander claimed on television that he had been denied dialysis because of his age. In reply, the Minister of Health pointed out that he also had serious coronary artery disease and prostate cancer, which had had to be taken into account when the decision was made.

Such limiting-of-care decisions are being made without any public discussion of the fact that the main reason they are made is the advances in medical techniques that enable the dying process to be so prolonged. But there is a striking exception to this 'let's bury our heads in the sand and hope the problem will go away' approach. In August 1996 the British Parliament was due to bring to an end the 'year and a day' rule that has been operating for 700 years. The law stated that a victim of a serious assault had to die of his injuries within a year and a day if his attacker were to be charged with murder. After that date, even though there could be no doubt that it was the attack that caused death, there could only be to a lesser charge. So violent criminals who had killed someone were sentenced for 'grievous bodily harm' and imprisoned for less than two years. The distress that this caused the relatives of the victims, and the offence it gave to common sense has brought about an unusually prompt change in the law to take account of the medical techniques that allow a victim's death to be postponed long after a year since the attack.

The just distribution of health resources, given that every possible life-prolonging treatment cannot be provided for everybody, will be a much more challenging problem for our social arrangements to resolve. Who is to decide on the priorities? What will the criteria be?

Before we look more closely at these questions, we must be clear that, as long as private health care is available, the rich will be able to buy all the medical treatment they want – or it may be that they will get as much as their relatives decree they shall have. In the case of national heads of state, it may be that political considerations will play a part. As we have noted, the fact that George V's death was deliberately brought forward by a few hours in order that the announcement could be first made to the nation in the most respected of the daily papers is well documented. That was in 1935.

In January 1989 the Japanese Emperor, Hirohito, died. He was nearly 88 years old. In the previous September he had suddenly vomited a large volume of blood and was very seriously ill for the remaining 111 days of his life. He was attended by five doctors and eight nurses; there were press conferences three times a day, giving details of his weight, blood pressure and the blood transfusions he was frequently being given. Officially, his disease was chronic pancreatitis, but everyone assumed it was cancer, although in Japan it is not the custom to tell the patient the truth if the disease is incurable. During this period there were no street parades, sports festivals or other public celebrations, and frivolous entertainments were postponed until after the death. There was endless discussion among the population in general of the Emperor's condition and treatment, and the result was a nine-fold increase in membership of the Japanese Society for Dying with Dignity (JSDD) over the following three years. JSDD is not campaigning for doctors to be allowed to give positive help to die; it wants the right to refuse futile treatment towards the end of life. The numbers joining JSDD suggest that the Japanese did not envy the long dying endured by their Emperor.

President Tito of Yugoslavia and General Franco of Spain also deteriorated very slowly and publicly as they died. More recently, in contrast, President Mitterand of France declared before his death that he had completed the French version of an advance directive. These leaders were not subject to the sharing out of national health resources that will apply to most of the rest of us. The allocation of national income to defence, education, health, social welfare and all the other expenditures necessary to keep the country going is, of course, made at the top level of national government, but, traditionally, in Britain at least, the total amount to be spent on health has been about as much detail as the general public has been given. How that total was shared out between hospitals and family doctors, between health education and preventive measures, between maternity services and geriatric care – all those decisions, and many more besides, have not been in the public domain.

There has been a vague expectation that everything medically possible would be available, and doctors have frequently claimed to have no duty beyond acting in the best interest of the patient being treated at the time. When a patient has been denied a particular treatment there has been public outcry, especially if that patient has been a young child, yet the knowledge that the ever-expanding number and complexity of medical techniques available cannot possibly be used universally is gradually seeping through. Doctors, after all, are part of a health-care team, and it is assumed that decisions will be discussed and shared. Few doctors are not involved in research or in-service training, and they are slowly having to face the facts that money cannot be spent twice, that a hospital bed allocated to one patient may mean longer on the waiting list for another – in short, that hard choices have to be made. Policy decisions have to be made in the sharing out of health resources, and great efforts must be made to provide rational and democratic ways of doing it. Let us look at just two of the possible systems.

The first tries to prioritize patients and their treatments by using Quality Adjusted Life Years (QALYs). Entire books have been written on the subject, but the basic idea is that the measure of the effectiveness of a proposed medical treatment should involve the quality of extra life it gives the patient as well as the quantity. It is possible, for example, that surviving for a long time in a grossly handicapped state would not rate as highly as having an enjoyable life for a shorter time. The earliest recipients of transplanted hearts, for instance, sometimes expressed this feeling during the time between getting the new heart and their deaths. But the cost of the procedures is also a factor. Giving many more cheap and simple treatments that improve things a good deal for a considerable number of people may have to be balanced against achieving a spectacular improvement for just one individual. The more one thinks about it, the more complicated and difficult it looks.

The state government of Oregon tried to draw up a system of health-care allocation by using a sort of referendum. Large numbers of citizens were asked to rank their preferences among the various ways that the money available for health care could be spent. The public did not specifically exclude the elderly from care, but it gave priority to maternity care and to preventive care for children. It also gave priority to acute fatal conditions if treatment would prevent death and lead to full recovery. Need, benefit and cost were therefore emphasized. It still wasn't easy to work out the spending plan, and when the first case to be denied a treatment according to that plan turned out to be a young child, an emotional television appeal raised the money on a charitable basis anyway! (Incidentally, it appears to be a pure coincidence that this happened in the same comparatively small American state as the passing of the Medical-Aid-in-Dying Act referred to in Chapter 7. The organizing bodies concerned are certainly entirely separate groups of people.)

While all these necessarily elaborate ways of sharing scarce health resources are debated, doctors are having to make daily decisions between competing claims. Perhaps if we were told on what basis they act, there could be public debate about what goes on and agreement on some basic principles might emerge from that discussion. Even if it did not, we would, as patients, have a better idea of what questions to ask.

In 1994 a consultant working in a hospital in Bradford, Yorkshire, published an article in the *Journal of Medical Ethics*. In it he defended the practice of ageism – that is, of taking the age of the patient into account when deciding on medical treatment – and he gave an example from his own hospital. Patients under the age of 65 who are admitted after a suspected heart attack go straight to the coronary care unit. Patients over the age of 65 go to a general ward and are transferred to the specialist unit only if their diagnosis is confirmed. The consultant wrote: 'Doctors have accepted this for many years as a just and effective way of using a limited resource. The public have never been consulted.'

It is worth noting that this 'Bradford' model does not deny treatment to the elderly, but it targets resources on younger patients. As long as the local population had been informed about the policy in simple enough language, the vast majority, including the elderly, would, no doubt, have accepted it as reasonable. What usually happens, however, is that an investigative journalist hears of a case where an older patient has allegedly suffered because of it. The distraught relatives are interviewed in the media, and no mention is ever made of the impossibility of providing ideal care for everyone. Presumably it is dread of this kind of publicity that encourages the authorities to make these rationing decisions in private.

The main drawback with all three of these possible approaches – QUALYs, Oregon public consultation and doctors' own guidelines – is that none of them looks at the problem from the patient's point of view, and any such discussion must take into account the fact that the general public is better informed than it used to be and getting steadily more so.

Television is probably the single most striking new addition to everyday living in the second half of this century compared with all previous ages. Not only does it enable us to know of events all over the world more or less as they happen, but it also shows us modes of life very different from our own. The contrast may lead to envy and resentment, or to an ambition to emulate another lifestyle, or to contentment with our lot. Whatever it is, we are better informed about all manner of things, including health issues. Although many people regard television as entertainment only, it is also a source of enlightenment and understanding. The level of knowledge by lay people of how their bodies work is now much higher than ever before. Awareness of what may go wrong and to what extent this can be avoided is also widespread – the link between a diet too high in animal fat and a wide range of health problems seems to be firmly established, for example.

There is another problem about a public discussion of the rationing of health care from the point of view of the health-care professionals and those in charge of the public purse, and this is that the patient is assumed to be grateful to accept whatever treatment the doctors offer or stoical if told that no treatment is available. Presumably this is because it is also assumed that the patient will eagerly accept any offered treatment, no matter how burdensome it may be and no matter how slight the benefit is likely to be. But we have already seen evidence that this is far from true: many people already think that those nearing the end of their lives should have the right not only to refuse all unwanted treatment but to have medical help to die as well, if necessary.

When people ask to be allowed to die of an incurable illness at a time they feel is right, the fact that medical resources will be released for the use of other patients may well be in their mind. As one person joining the Voluntary Euthanasia Society wrote: 'I couldn't bear to lie there, longing for the end, and knowing that the hospital bed I was occupying could be used by someone who was going to get better.' Another said:

When I decide my life is over and I'd like to say goodbye to my

*family and go to sleep for the last time, it's going to give me
such pleasure that someone is going to benefit from the weeks
of medical care I'm gladly releasing. It will be like deciding I
have no further use for what used to be my favourite garment,
then giving it to a charity shop instead of putting it in the dust-
bin.*

Both those people were imagining their possible future, but it
happens in reality, too. In 1988 in Greece a family of four, one
brother and three sisters, aged between 74 and 82, gassed
themselves because they did not want to be a burden to others.
There was no suggestion that proper care would not have been
available to them had they chosen to make use of it. Six years
later a Florida couple facing old age and disease, ended their
lives together to avoid squandering their fortune on health
care. They had left their $10,000,000 to charity.

In Britain there are estimated to be between 1,000 and 1,500
patients in a persistent vegetative state. A television programme brought responses from 78 families that have had relatives in this state for more than ten years. The costs of the
treatment run into many millions of pounds, and similar
figures would probably emerge in every country where
advanced modern medicine is practised. The waste of nursing
and medical skills that could be used to benefit other patients
with some hope of recovery may add to the distress of the families involved.

Considering the welfare of others is something that normal
people do throughout their lives, even if that concern is confined to members of the immediate family, and being unselfish
used to be regarded as the prime virtue. In fact, accepting
without question the use of health resources seems to be the
only occasion on which society expects, indeed demands, that
we think only of ourselves. It is necessary that individuals
should be encouraged not to be too self-sacrificing, of course,
but there is a difference between that and denying them the
right to be altruistic. Getting very old and parting gradually

with one's mobility, sight and hearing is bad enough. Being deprived also of one's natural inclination to altruism seems to be piling on the agony.

Not wanting to be a burden on others is closely linked with the prospect of depending on others for the mechanics of everyday life. Surveys of the elderly consistently record their intense dislike of the prospect of losing their independence. Being unable to feed oneself, to dress and undress unaided, to keep oneself clean and, above all, to attend to one's own toileting – all these are felt to involve a loss of dignity, and it is useless for those who devote their lives to geriatric care or medicine to assert that their patients live dignified and valuable lives. Whether our life has dignity is a judgement we all make for ourselves – as long as we are capable of rational thought. Some people face with serenity the thought of spending their last years, possibly very many years, needing total care. Many do not. Shakespeare's seventh age of man

> *second childishness and mere oblivion*
> *Sans teeth, sans eyes, sans taste, sans everything*

is the stage of life that most would rather forgo, or at the very least, be allowed to cut short.

There is no way of knowing whether the numbers of people choosing to forgo a long period of dependency at the end of their lives would be high enough to have any significant effect. When a well-organized system of advance directives was introduced in Denmark a few years ago, the authorities were unprepared for the demand – it was three times the anticipated level.

Until quite recently it was taken for granted that men would occupy nearly all the powerful, decision-making positions in the state, and that women would accept this contentedly. This is still the position in many parts of the world, but less so with every passing year, and there is no reason to think the progress of women's emancipation will stop. This phenomenon is yet another that tends towards the acceptance of legalizing choice in dying. This is partly because, on average, women live longer than men and thus form the greater proportion of those living on, often unwillingly, into a frail and dependent old age. The majority of the law-makers, senior legal figures and heads of the medical profession on the other hand, are men. Moreover they tend to be from those classes of society in which the men have never been expected to be domestically independent. The prospect of dependency is not so abhorrent to them as it is to most women.

One other element in modern life and one that is linked with a higher standard of living and with being better informed in general is an increased desire for autonomy. People become less and less willing to accept that those in authority should have the right to impose decisions on them about their personal affairs. In the field of end-of-life decisions this can be very easily seen in the rapid growth worldwide of the right-to-die movement. When the first few societies formed a World Federation in 1980 there were 12 of them; now there are 40. The European Division of this Federation alone has 14 member societies, representing 200,000 individuals. The subject of voluntary euthanasia is more and more frequently discussed in the media, and public sympathy is overwhelmingly in favour of recognizing patients' rights to remain in control up to the end of their lives.

At the time of the trial of Dr Cox, an editorial in the *British Medical Journal* said:

The mood of the nation seems to be that the conviction may have been legally correct but that to destroy a caring doctor through such a trial was wrong. The law is in effect the codification of the will of the people, and when there is such tension between a legal verdict and the people's thinking then it is time to reconsider the law.

So far the government has not responded, but the next

Parliament may be more inclined to innovation, so even in Britain legal reform may start to happen.

It is, however, in the newer democracies of North America and Australia that legal progress has already started and is likely in the near future to continue to be ahead of the rest of the world.

In giving frail old people the right not to have their lives medically extended against their wishes we would be returning to an acceptance of death as a natural final life event, rather than as something to be desperately fought against. All pre-industrial societies had some mechanism for shortening the period of total dependency at the end of life. In times of great food shortage, the dependent old were the first to go short, simply because the whole tribe would perish if the food-producers of the present and the future were allowed to starve. The best known and most dramatic example of this is the Inuit custom of putting old people out on the ice to die of hypothermia. The reason for doing this was obvious to everyone, and the old accepted it as just.

The shortages that we industrialized peoples of today will increasingly face are not of food or basic necessities. They are of sophisticated, life-prolonging medical treatments. Patients must be more fully involved in the decisions to give or abstain from them, and if a patient is no longer capable of playing a part in the decision-making process – and the increasing use of advance directives will help to mitigate this difficulty – the carers must make every effort to consider the patient as a person, not simply as the embodiment of a medical problem.

The following statistics, for example, give pause for thought. In Britain in 1994 hip operations, mainly involving the replacement of the joint, were performed on 2,226 people aged between 90 and 94, on 492 people aged between 95 and 99, and on 29 people who were more than 100 years old. Possibly all these people chose to have this done and benefited enough to judge that their quality of life was significantly improved. One would like to be sure.

Two years earlier a report by the medical colleges noted:

There are roughly 3 million operations each year and about 18,000 of those patients die within 30 days. These deaths are almost entirely restricted to the very old and the very sick. Surgery should be avoided for those whose death is inevitable and imminent. A more humane approach to the care of these patients should be considered.

We are now reaching what turns out to have been a quite short period in human history – a time when our medical resources match our mastery of medical techniques. From this period on we shall have to choose which of the available medical treatments it will be appropriate to offer to which patients. It is vital that a good system of voluntary euthanasia is set up at the outset. If the decisions about who gets what are left entirely to professionals, that will amount to involuntary euthanasia for the people who are required to forgo life-prolonging treatment.

Controlling the circumstances of our dying on the basis of rational decisions should not be regarded as a backward step. This is true for the individual and for policy decisions that enable health resources to be shared out with justice. Birth control was bitterly opposed until the middle of this century, but the ability to choose how many children we produce is now a human right that we take for granted. It is easy to forget the miseries that multiple pregnancies and unwanted children can impose on the poor.

At the other end of life, the right to decide for ourselves when to retire from life's stage and to have medical help to do it gracefully will be a similar improvement. Mankind will be taking responsibility for its own fertility.

Further Reading

Dworkin, Ronald, *Life's Dominion*, HarperCollins Publishers, London 1993
The philosophical arguments are expounded with great clarity.

Humphry, Derek, and Wickett, Ann , *The Right to Die*, Bodley Head, London, 1986
The most comprehensive account of the voluntary euthanasia movement up to 1986.

Humphry, Derek, *Final Exit*, Hemlock Society, 1991
A handbook on self-deliverance that became a best-seller in the United States.

Keizer, Bert, *Dancing with Mister D*, Transworld Publishers Ltd, London, 1996
Written (and translated) by a Dutch doctor working in a Dutch nursing home. The author has changed the names and circumstances of his patients to protect their confidentiality, but he writes sensitively about them and is entertaining, too. A masterpiece.

Kennedy Ludovic, *Euthanasia: the Good Death*, Chatto & Windus, London, 1990
One of a series under the general heading 'Counterblasts', in which 'Britain's finest writers and thinkers confront the crucial issues of the day'.

Keown, John (ed.), *Euthanasia Examined*, Cambridge University Press, Cambridge, 1995
A collection of essays by 14 contributors, the majority of whom argue against legalizing voluntary euthanasia.

Larue, Gerald, *Playing God: 50 Religions' Views on Your Right to Die*, Moyer Bell, London, 1996

The subtitle explains the book's purpose.

Logue, Barbara J., *Last Rights*, Macmillan Inc., New York, 1993

Looks at the question of humanity's control of birth and death on a large timescale and worldwide, as befits a demographer.

Innumerable articles have also appeared in the various medical, legal and philosophical academic journals. Medical ethics has its own literature, which includes much discussion of end-of-life issues. The best known of these are, in Britain, *The Journal of Medical Ethics* and, in the United States, *The Hastings Center Report*.

The internet has several sites giving up-to-date information.

The Voluntary Euthanasia Society (VES) may be contacted at:

13 Prince of Wales Terrace
London W8 5PG
tel: 0171 937 7770
fax: 0171 376 2648
e-mail: ves.london@dial.pipex.com

The VES holds audio and video tapes on all aspects of voluntary euthanasia.

Index